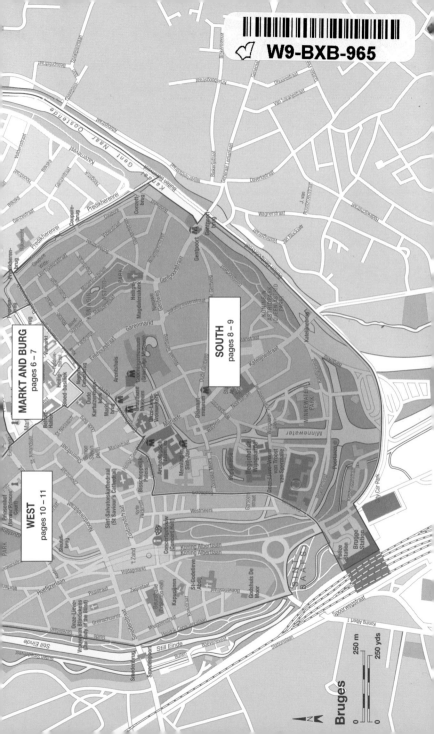

INSIGHT GUIDES

BRUGES
smart guide

APA PUBLICATIONS
Part of the Langenscheidt Publishing Group

Contents

Below: Vedett is just one of the many local beers you can try while in Bruges.

VEDETT
EXTRA BLOND
PENGUINS KNOW WHY
VEDETT.COM

Below: detail from the ornate Oude Griffie.

3

Bruges

Bruges is a Gothic gem of a city that has seen good and bad times, and lived to tell the tale. Its glittering years as a commercial hotspot – from 1200 to 1400 – were followed by decline after its sea route silted up. Disaster back then has brought riches today: having lain untouched for centuries it has become a living museum; a symbol of the modern Flemish renaissance.

Bruges Facts and Figures

Population: **Central Bruges 20,000 (entire municipal area including suburbs, villages and Zeebrugge: 117,000)**
Area: **4.3 sq km (municipal area: 138.4 sq km)**
Population density: **5,000 inhabitants per sq km**
Number of nationalities resident in Bruges: **136**
Visitors staying overnight in central Bruges: **1.45 million per year**
No. of hotel rooms: **over 3,000**
No. of World Heritage Sites: **3 (entire city centre, Belfry and Begijnhof)**
No. of museums: **25**
No. of bridges: **30**
No. of churches: **15**
No. of restaurants with Michelin stars: **7**

Geography

Bruges – *Brugge* to its residents – is situated where the polders of the maritime plain meet the sandy interior of Flanders. It is capital of West Flanders, one of Belgium's 11 provinces, bordered by the Netherlands, France, the North Sea (it contains the entire Belgian coastline), the Walloon province of Hainaut and the Flemish province of East Flanders.

Its egg-shaped historic centre is contained by a 7km-long 'ring canal', which traces the route of the former defensive outer ramparts. Within this boundary are all the visitor attractions and most tourist accommodation. A ring road follows this perimeter boundary and keeps most traffic well away from the centre, which has a traffic management policy (one-way streets) designed to discourage motorists, and where most people move around on foot or by bicycle.

The city suburbs are named after parishes outside the old walls (Sint-Michiels, Sint-Andries, Sint-Jozef, Sint-Pieters, Sint-Kruis and so on). The municipal district of Bruges includes these outskirts, as well as a stretch of land between Bruges and the coast, encompassing the historic village of Lissewege and the port-town of Zeebrugge, which is linked to the city by canal.

Rivers and Canals

The renown of Bruges is rooted deep in its waterways. The city grew up from a Gallo-Roman settlement on the banks of the rivers Dijver and Reie. It is first mentioned by name in 864, when the name *Bruggia* – meaning 'landing stage', or 'port' – appears on coins.

Until the 11th century, ships could sail right into the city along the River Reie. By that time, the development of the cloth industry had made the city an international trading hub. Silting closed access by the end of the century, but a new channel was created by a coastal flood in 1134. This channel – Het Zwin – reopened a sea route as far as Damme, north-east of Bruges. A canal was dug to Damme, and this became the city's commercial outpost.

Below: a horse-drawn tour of the Markt.

The Zwin outlet silted up again from the early 16th century, sealing the end of the city's golden age, but the remaining canal network has cemented Bruge's reputation, and explains the oft-heard title, 'the Venice of the North'.

From Hunger to Tourism

If it rose to prominence thanks to its weaving and waters, Bruges retains its pristine condition thanks to early tourists. The advent of the railway connecting Ostend, Bruges, Ghent and Brussels reversed the poverty-stricken town's fortunes, as Britons en route to visit the Waterloo battlefields 'discovered' a city preserved in time. Word spread and tentative conservation efforts were begun. Now the town is a pocket-sized museum piece, peopled by camera-wielding visitors.

Population

The West Flemish are famously unfriendly, and speak a dialect that even other Flemings find hard to understand, yet they are intensely proud of their provincial capital and lay on a fine spread for the thousands of tourists who come to visit each day. As the Flemish economy thrives, and Bruges scrubs its bricks cleaner with every passing year, valiant efforts are being made to strike a balance between the 21st century city, as represented by the daring new Concertgebouw, and the time capsule on which its current fortune depends.

Highlights

▲ **Groeningemuseum** The provincial city art gallery with a world-class reputation.
▶ **Memling in Sint-Jan** Jewel-like colours and the finest detail characterise the Memling masterpieces.

▶ **Belfort and Hallen** The great Belfry and Market Hall, built in the 13th century and as impressive now as they were then.

▲ **Burg** The city grew from this original square, now a panorama of architectural history that includes the revered Holy Blood basilica.

▲ **Begijnhof de Wijngaarde** Maybe the best surviving example of a *beguinage*, dating from medieval times.
▶ **Canals** The lifeblood of the city and magnetic in their attraction.

Markt and Burg

The energy of Bruges comes from its two central squares, the Markt and the Burg, representing the historic city's dual strengths: trade and nobility. The Burg is older and grander: a fortified castle was built here in the 9th century and the city grew up around it. It remained the seat of the Counts of Flanders until the dukes of Burgundy decamped to Prinsenhof palace in the 15th century, and the square is still full of architectural treasures. The Markt was the heart of commercial activity: goods were traded in the Hallen; and the trades' guildhouses – now busy pavement cafés – surround the square. There is a food market here every Wednesday.

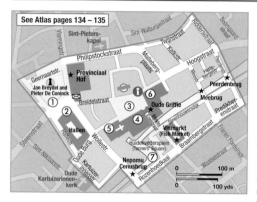

See Atlas pages 134 – 135

The Markt ①

The Markt has been the hub of daily life in Bruges for over 1,000 years, having served as a marketplace since 958. It is still the focal point of commercial activity, and hosts markets, festivities and street entertainment. Buses and cyclists rattle across the cobbles, and horse-drawn carriage tours depart from here.

Dominating the square is the 13th-century brick complex of the **Belfort-Hallen** ②, the Belfry from which a carillon chimes every quarter-hour. The former cloth halls around its base are where merchants would come to trade their wares.

On the east side of the square stand the city's main

post office and the neo-Gothic **Provinciaal Hof**, the seat of the provincial government of West Flanders. This was previously the site of the Waterhalle (Water Hall), which covered a central canal dock and large quaysides. Cargo would be loaded and unloaded from small boats, which arrived heavily laden from Damme, the city's former sea-port 7km (4 miles) north-east of Bruges. The canal was later truncated to end at Jan Van Eyckplein.

The **statue** at the centre of the Markt honours two heroes of the Flemish rebellion against the French at the Battle of the Golden Spurs in 1302, named Jan Breydel and Pieter De Coninck.

SEE ALSO MONUMENTS, P.78

The Burg ③

The most historic square in Bruges, referred to in manuscripts from the 9th century, the Burg was the centre of civic and religious life, leaving the grubby business of commerce to the Markt. It takes its name from the fortress or 'burg' that was built here in 865 by Baldwin Iron Arm, the first Count of Flanders, as a defence against Norman invasion, and around which a village developed. Popular events, including burnings at the stake and beheadings, were often held in the Burg. Today, you are more likely to see an outdoor concert.

Pride of place goes to the graceful, triple-turreted Gothic **Stadhuis** ④ (City

Below: Justice holds her scales atop the Proosdij in the Burg.

Left: a row of restaurants
lining the Markt.

rent structure built in 1821 and still partly occupied by fresh fish stalls each morning except Sunday. Next to it are the Huidenvettersplein (Tanners' Square), which was surrounded by the tanners' guildhouse (built in 1523 and turreted) and the Fishmongers' Corporation House (beside the boat trip booth and jetty; note the fishy coat of arms above the door, *see* picture below). Crossing Tanners' Square diagonally, you reach **Rozenhoedkaai** ⑦ (Rosary Quay), where the low canal wall provides ample room to enjoy one of the most popular viewpoints in Bruges: across a broad sweep of canal and a cluster of tiled rooftops to the Belfry.

SEE ALSO CANALS AND BRIDGES, P.38

Groenerei

A left turn at the Vismarkt takes you along the lovely Groenerei canalside, where two pretty bridges, the Meebrug and Peerdenbrug, offer a view back to the rear of the Stadhuis and the tower of Sint-Salvatorskathedraal.

Below: coat of arms on the former Fishmongers' Corporation House.

Hall), on the south side of the square. This late 14th-century building was built on the site of a former prison. In the south-west corner of the Burg is the **Heilig Bloedbasiliek** ⑤ (Basilica of the Holy Blood), two chapels one atop of the other built in honour of a sacred relic: a phial alleged to contain Christ's blood, brought back from the Holy Land in the 12th century. On the other side of the Stadhuis is the **Oude Griffie** (1537), the old county records office now occupied by law courts. Next door, in the south-east corner of the square, stands the large neoclassical **Paleis van Het Brugse Vrije** ⑥ (Liberty of Bruges Palace), seat of an autonomous administrative district (the Brugse Vrije) created in the 12th century, which included much of Flanders but not Bruges. The Palace was rebuilt in the 18th century on the site of the 1520s original, parts of which can be seen from the canalside of the building.

SEE ALSO ARCHITECTURE, P.25; CHURCHES, P.46; MONUMENTS, P.81; MUSEUMS AND GALLERIES, P.82

Vismarkt and Huidenvettersplein

Along Blinde Ezelstraat and across the canal you are transported from the rarefied realm of nobles and religious relics to daily life in medieval Bruges. Across the canal, which would have served as an open drain, is the Vismarkt (fish market) – the cur-

Horse-and-carriage tours of Bruges leave from the Markt every day from 9.30am–5.30pm, except during the Wednesday street market, when the carriages redeploy to the Burg, and during icy weather. A tour lasts around 35 minutes and costs €35 for up to five adults.

South

Bruges is at its most seductive in the lush south of the city. The district south of the Dijver feels far removed from the outside world and its commercial imperatives, and the treasures in its museums and churches seem to stand aloof from the wealth that brought them into being. Some of the world's greatest artworks are here: Van Dycks in the Groeninge-museum, Memlings in the former hospital of Sint-Jan, and a Michelangelo in the Onze-Lieve-Vrouwekerk. Further south is the Begijnhof, a medieval community for women, and the Minnewater park with its lake and swans, where you could be forgiven for imagining that you are on a film set.

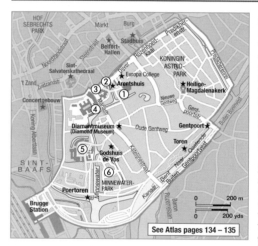

See Atlas pages 134 – 135

Groeningemuseum ①

Built in 1929 on the site of a former Augustinian monastery, and restored in 2002–3, the city's most important – and moderately sized – museum was designed to house works which had formerly been dis-played in the Bruges Academy of Fine Arts. Many of the older works date from the Golden Age of Bruges, and were com-missioned by the city's wealthy burghers, merchants and clerics, several of whom appear in the biblical scenes depicted. An extension of the museum, used for temporary exhibitions and to house the

city's collection of works by Belgo-British artist Frank Brangwyn, is in the **Arentshuis**, an 18th-century mansion across the cobbled lane (called Groeninge).
SEE ALSO MUSEUMS AND GALLERIES, P.83, 85

Gruuthuse Museum ②

Further along the Dijver past the Arentshuis is the lavish 15th-century Palace of the Lords of Gruuthuse, built by a family who had a lucrative monopoly on the sale of *gruut* (a mixture of herbs for improving the flavour of beer), and later held the tax

concession on beer itself. Its leading light was Lodewijk van Gruuthuse (*c.*1427–92), counsellor to the Burgun-dian dukes Philip the Good and Charles the Bold, whose equestrian statue stands sentinel above the entrance. Today it is a museum of decorative arts.
SEE ALSO MUSEUMS AND GALLERIES, P.86

Onze-Lieve-Vrouwekerk ③

Abutting the palace is the **Onze-Lieve-Vrouwekerk** (Church of Our Lady), whose vast brick tower and spire – the second highest in Bel-gium – dominates the city beneath. First mentioned in records in 1089, it once served as a kind of inland

Below: the Groeningemuseum is housed in a former monastery.

Left: romantic Minnewater with its Lake of Love.

Next door to the Groeninge-museum is the main building of the College of Europe, an elite post-university establishment founded in 1949 to drive the unification of Europe. Today, 400 graduates, who must be conversant in French and English, follow one-year Masters programmes in law, economics or political science, in preparation for a high-flying career in the European institutions or international business. The college also has a campus in Warsaw (Natolin), opened in 1992 (www.coleurop.be).

lighthouse for ships on their way to Bruges. The church's main attractions are a Michelangelo sculpture and the tombs of Mary of Burgundy, who died in 1482, and her father, Charles the Bold, who died in 1477. It was in this church that Mary married Maximilian of Austria in 1477, joining the house of Burgundy to the Habsburgs, in a ceremony noted for its lavishness and for the fact that the bride and groom could not speak each other's language.
SEE ALSO CHURCHES, P.47; MUSEUMS AND GALLERIES, P.86

Memling in Sint-Jan ④

The floor level is a metre below the road behind the Gothic doorway of the **Memling in Sint-Jan** museum, showing how the street level has risen over the centuries. The museum contains priceless works by German artist Hans Memling, who came to Bruges aged 25 and made his fortune, becoming one of the richest men in the city by the time he died here in 1494. Six of his paintings can be seen in the former chapel of the **Sint-Janshospitaal** (St John's hospital), founded in the 12th century. It is now a fascinating hospital museum.
SEE ALSO MUSEUMS AND GALLERIES, P.87

Begijnhof De Wijngaarde

South down the canal from Sint-Janshospitaal, following the winding streets, is the enclosure of the **begijnhof** ⑤, a grassy tree-shaded courtyard surrounded by whitewashed houses that were occupied by women (beguines) who renounced wealth but did not take holy orders. The last beguine left in 1927, and the site is now owned by a Benedictine convent whose nuns wear habits similar to those worn by the beguines. Many of the houses are now occupied by lay people, but the convent maintains a guest house for those on spiritual visits.
SEE ALSO BEGUINAGES, P.29; MUSEUMS AND GALLERIES, P.84

Parks

Two of the city's largest green spaces are in the south: the pretty **Minnewater park** ⑥, with its large lake (the so-called 'Lake of Love'), and east, the landscaped former botanical garden of **Koningin Astridpark** (Queen Astrid Park).
SEE ALSO PARKS AND GARDENS, P.105

Below: tranquility in the courtyard of the begijnhof.

West

The Burgundian dukes made this district their home in the 15th century. Nearby Sint-Jakobskerk did well out of it, as princes and merchants sought to out-do each other in generosity to their parish church. Later, the cathedral of Bruges moved to the west, after the original in the Burg was destroyed. Today, the area is mainly visited for the two long shopping streets that run parallel to each other from the Markt to the 't Zand square, site of a former railway station and now dominated by the city's new concert hall. Beyond that lies a quiet district of respectable terraced houses, including a pretty street lined with typical almshouses.

See Atlas pages 132 & 134

Prinsenhof ①

The Kempinski Dukes' Palace luxury hotel occupies the site of the former Burgundian palace, the **Prinsenhof** (Princes' Court), built for the dukes of Burgundy to replace their damp and draughty 11th-century wooden residence on the Burg. The original palace – what survives is a largely rebuilt, neo-Gothic copy – was

---

A delicate statue of Mary of Burgundy riding side-saddle on a horse, *Flandria Nostra*, is situated on Muntplein, not far from the Prinsenhof.

---

vast: it would have been surrounded by high walls and battlements and stretched from Noordzandstraat to the parallel Moerstraat.

Philip the Good married Isabella of Portugal here in 1430, and founded the Order of the Golden Fleece to mark the event. The wedding banquet was held in a hall decorated with tapestries made of gold thread specially for the occasion. Every dish was delivered on a gold platter, to the sound of trumpets, while jousting entertained the guests outside. Philip's son Duke Charles the Bold married Margaret of York here in 1468, again with the kind of banquet that has made the term 'Burgundian' a byword for excess. Sorrow began to

shroud the palace after the violent death of Charles the Bold, in 1477. Just five years later, Charles' daughter Mary, Duchess of Burgundy, died in the palace as a result of injuries sustained during a riding accident. She was just 25. Her death led to widespread mourning, and the building never recovered its former glory. The Habsburgs put it up for sale in 1631, and it passed into the hands of a Franciscan order, before being largely destroyed under French rule at the end of the 18th century.

Sint-Jakobskerk ②

The 13th-century church was enlarged due to gifts from the dukes of Burgundy and then packed with valuable artworks by wealthy donors; it

Below: bronze sculpture of bathing women on the 't Zand.

Left: lively brasseries around the bustling 't Zand.

From 1424 until his death in 1441, painter Jan Van Eyck was in the pay of Philip the Good, Duke of Burgundy. A member of the diplomatic mission sent to Lisbon in 1428 to beg the hand of Isabella of Portugal, it is said that his portrait of her helped confirm the duke's choice of wife. He also undertook a number of secret missions for the duke, for which he was handsomely rewarded.

by funfairs and a Saturday market, and lined with cafés and brasseries frequented more by locals than tourists. The vista is now dominated by the remarkable modern **Concertgebouw** ⑤ (concert hall), created in 2002 for the city's year as European Capital of Culture.
SEE ALSO ARCHITECTURE, P.24

Almshouses

West of 't Zand is a calm, residential neighbourhood with a number of *godshuizen* (almshouses), particularly along Boeveriestraat, where the tiny whitewashed homes have been undergoing renovation for 21st century occupants: the **Godshuis De Moor** was founded in 1480 for aged stonemasons, carpenters and coopers; while **Godshuis Van Volden** occupies the site of a medieval hospital for foundlings and mentally ill children. A little to the north, clustered around the chapel of **Onze-Lieve Vrouw van Blindekens** ⑥ (Our Lady of the Blind) on Kreupelenstraat, are almshouses for the blind: named Van Pamel, Marius Voet and Laurentia Soutieu.
SEE ALSO CHURCHES, P.48;
PALACES AND HOUSES, P.101

Although the chapel buildings date from the 17th century, Onze-Lieve-Vrouw van Blindekens (Our Lady of the Blind) was built to honour a promise made at the battle of Mons-en-Pévèle in 1304 against the French (which resulted in a treaty granting Flemish independence). The chapel is the departure point for the annual Feast of the Assumption procession held on 15 August, which makes its way from here to Onze-Lieve-Vrouw van de Potterie (Our Lady of the Pottery), on Potterierei.

has an internal harmony lacking in many Bruges churches and is lit by a pale pink light when the sun shines.
SEE ALSO CHURCHES, P.48

Sint-Salvatorskathedraal

During the Burgundian era, **Sint-Salvatorskathedraal** ③ was just St Saviour's, another parish church, albeit the oldest in Bruges, dating from the 9th century. When Bruges found itself a cathedral-free zone, after French occupation forces demolished St Donatian's Cathedral in the Burg, St Saviour's was pressed into service in 1834 as a replacement seat for the Bishop of Bruges. The **museum** in its treasury contains valuable artworks, and the 15th-century wooden choir stalls flanking the altar bear a complete set of escutcheons of the Knights of the Order of the Golden Fleece, who held a chapter meeting here in 1478.
SEE ALSO CHURCHES, P.49;
MUSEUMS AND GALLERIES, P.88

't Zand ④

Major transformations on the **'t Zand** in recent years have given a new burst of life to this once dreary square, left vacant when the city's first railway station moved south. The ring road passes under the square, which is cheered

North

Northern Bruges was historically the city's gateway to the outside world, via the canal to Damme and the Zwin inlet. Merchants from all over Europe set up trading posts locally, and their legacy lives on in street names like Spanjaardstraat (Spanish Street), Engelsestraat (English Street) and Oosterlingenplein (Easterners' Square), which referred to the German traders based here. Beyond this distinctly grand quarter, and the other side of a wonderful stretch of canal, is the old artists' neighbourhood of Sint-Gillis (Saint Giles). It is centred around the Gothic church of Sint Gillis and pleasantly removed from the tourist frenzy of other areas.

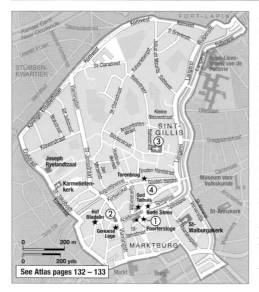

See Atlas pages 132 – 133

Jan Van Eyckplein ①

During the Middle Ages, when Bruges was a key member of the powerful Baltic-based Hanseatic League trading alliance, hosting the most important of the league's principal *kontore* (foreign outposts), this square was a busy place. On the west side is the slender-towered **Poortersloge** (Burghers' Lodge), something of an elite gentlemen's club in the 15th century, now

home to the town archives. On the north side of the square is the **Oud Tolhuis** (Customs House), where taxes were levied on imported goods, and next to it the tiny *pijnders* (porters) lodge. The two buildings are now part of the provincial library, and house hundreds of Gothic manuscripts. The **Rode Steen** house on the east of the square (Jan van Eyckplein 8) dates from the 13th–18th century; it was the

first house in Bruges to win renovation funding in the 19th century, marking the start of efforts to preserve the city's medieval character.

The two quays flanking the canal along Spiegelrei and Spinolarei were used as mooring points for boats arriving in the city, and mansions were built to house merchants and courtiers from other trading nations; many of the houses had vaulted cellars for storage, some of which can still be seen.
SEE ALSO MONUMENTS, P.79

Huis Ter Beurze ②

At Vlamingstraat 35 is **Huis Ter Beurze** (Ter Beurze House), with a plaque noting the year 1453 on the facade. It used to be an inn and money-changing operation run by the Van den Beurze family, and was frequented by so many foreign merchants and bankers that the surroundings became known as the Beur-splein. It is from this that the word 'Bourse', the common international name for a stock exchange, comes.

Several houses were occupied by Italian merchants: the **Genuese loge** (Genoese lodge) at Vlamingstraat 33 (1399), now the Friet Museum, has the city's

Left: Hans Memling looking down on Woensdagmarkt.

and was buried in **Sint-Gilliskerk** ③ in 1494. Lancelot Blondeel and Pieter Pourbus lived on the same street, while Gerard David and Antoon Claeissens lived on Sint-Jorisstraat. Jan van Eyck entertained guests in his home and studio at the junction of Torenbrug and Gouden-Hand-straat, overlooking the attractive stretch of canal along **Gouden-Handrei** ④.

The neighbourhood later became something of an English colony. An orphanage on Sint-Jorisstraat was run by an English family until World War I and an English seminary was located on Gouden Handstraat. The house on the corner of Sint-Jorisstraat and Clarastraat was owned by English art historian James Weale (1832–1917), who, together with poet Guido Gezelle, launched a magazine and is credited with rediscovering and identifying the works of Hans Memling and many other **Flemish Primitives**. SEE ALSO PAINTING AND SCULPTURE, P.96

Bruges' early prosperity was a result of its role as the chief port of Flanders, a hub of English and Scandinavian trade. From the Roman period to the 11th century, ships sailed right into the centre on the River Reie; later, sea-going ships sailed into Damme, while smaller vessels ferried goods along the canal from Damme to Bruges. In addition to being a major hub, Bruges was one of the important textile centres in north-west Europe.

Sint-Gillis

North of the canal that loops around this central northern area are the humble terraced streets of Sint-Gillis (St Giles) and Sint-Joris (St George), once home to the greatest names in Flemish painting. **Hans Memling** owned two houses on Jan Miraelstraat

coat of arms above the side door; there was also the **Venetian consulate** at number 37; and the **Florentine Lodge** at Academiestraat 1, now De Florentijnen restaurant. An engraving on the facade quotes a passage from Dante's *Divine Comedy* referring to Bruges. Not far away, the **Hof Bladelin** at Naaldenstraat 19 was home to Medici bank officials.

Below: peaceful stretch of water at Gouden Handrei.

East

The Sint-Anna district to the north-east of Bruges has a less worldly air than the rest of the city, its streets disturbed only by the sounds of bicycle bells, windmill sails or the lick of a paintbrush as the area completes its renovation. The museums here deal more with matters of everyday life – medicine in medieval Bruges, schooling and local crafts, lace-making and literature – while an unusual church recreates a corner of the Holy Land in Bruges. At the area's perimeter, the grassy banks of the canal ring – from the Coupure canal in the south-east to the Dampoort in the north – are popular with joggers, cyclists and dog-walkers.

See Atlas pages 133 & 135

Sint-Anna

Home in the 19th century to the poorest citizens, the streets around Sint-Annakerk were rediscovered by artists and, later, young professionals, who have restored the rows of terraced houses. There are few shops in the tranquil neighbourhood, which has something of a village atmosphere. The **Sint-**

Right: coat-of-arms finely crafted in lace.

Annakerk ① (Church of St Anne), with lavish decoration, is a 1624 baroque replacement for the Gothic church demolished in 1561.

The striking **Jeruzalemkerk** ② (Jerusalem Church) was built in 1428 by a wealthy Bruges family and modelled on the Church of the Holy Sepulchre in Jerusalem. Even stranger inside than out, the church is still privately owned, along with the **Kantcentrum** (Lace Centre) next door in 15th-century almshouses founded by the Adornes family.

The **Bruggemuseum-Volkskunde** ③ (Folklore Museum) recreates typical 19th-century interiors in a row of tiny almshouses along Balstraat, including workshops of various trades and craftspeople, a schoolroom and a tavern.
SEE ALSO CHILDREN, P.44; CHURCHES, P.50–1; MUSEUMS AND GALLERIES, P.89, 90–1

Around the Windmills

Out towards the ring canal are four wooden-stilt **windmills**, which remain from the 29 mills that once ringed the city ramparts. Two of them

Lace-making was an industry which at its peak in the 1840s provided steady employment – and low wages – for 10,000 local women and girls (nearly a quarter of the population). Handmade lace is expensive, and most of the lace sold today is machine-made and imported. The most popular kind made here is bobbin lace, created using a technique where threads of silk, linen or cotton on as many as 700 bobbins are crossed and braided around a framework of pins.

are open to the public in summer: regular demonstrations of the miller's craft prove that they are still in working order.

Nearby are the homes of two exclusive sporting clubs dating from the 16th century: the **Schuttersgilde Sint-Joris** and **Sint-Sebastiaan** (St George and St Sebastian Archers' Guilds), the first is

Left: 19th-century windmill Sint-Janshuismolen.

Dampoort, where the canal from Damme enters the city. This was the route by which trading vessels arrived in the Middle Ages. Today, pleasure cruisers and working barges wait here for the road-bridge to lift. After the route via the Zwin inlet and Damme silted up, a canal was built to Ostend, opened in 1622. Large vessels today generally take the Boudewijnkanaal to the sea port of Zeebrugge.

The canal snakes its way from here to the city centre along the tree-lined Potterierei, named after the chapel of the potters' guild, the **Onze-Lieve-Vrouw ter Potterie** ⑤ (Our Lady of the Pottery), and its adjacent hospice, dating from 1276 and functioning until the 17th century. Parts of the former hospice now house the **Potterie-museum**, dedicated to the history of medical treatment, as well as furniture, paintings and religious artefacts.

A little further down the canal is the baroque church and college of the **Groot Seminarie**, the episcopal seminary, which occupies the former Duinen Abdij (Abbey of the Dunes).
SEE ALSO CHURCHES, P.51; MONUMENTS, P.81; MUSEUMS AND GALLERIES, P.91

Around Langestraat

The neighbourhood south of Langestraat, bordered to the west by the **Coupure** canal, was until recently a forgotten corner of the city. Gentrification has recently arrived, and the streets are newly cobbled and dotted with quiet bed and breakfast places. The quayside along **Predikherenrei** is a mooring spot for houseboats.
SEE ALSO CANALS AND BRIDGES, P.38

Fluent in English, the poet and priest Guido Gezelle translated several English works into Dutch. He also catalogued around 150,000 words, phrases and proverbial sayings from the old Netherlandic dialect and wrote poetry that aimed to recreate the 'golden age' of Flanders' rural and devoutly Catholic society.

for the crossbow, the second for the longbow. Still with an elite – and all male – membership, they occupy historic buildings with fine gardens.

Between the clubs, on Rolweg, the **Bruggemuseum-Gezelle** ④ honours the work of the Bruges poet and priest (1830–99) in the house where he grew up. Gezelle was one of the principal 19th-century Flemish men of letters, and founder of the Flemish Academy of Language and Literature. He died in the **Engels Klooster** (English Convent) in the parallel street, Carmersstraat. The convent was one of the focal points of the English Colony, which in the 1860s numbered 1,200.
SEE ALSO MONUMENTS, P.80; MUSEUMS AND GALLERIES, P.90

Potterierei and Dampoort

The northernmost windmill, **Koeleweimolen** (Cool Meadow Mill), is up near the

Below. handsome buildings along the Potterierei.

Around Bruges

A ttractions outside central Bruges vary from the pretty villages of Damme and Lissewege to the north-east and north, the Boudewijn theme park with dolphinarium to the south and two country estates, Beisbroek and Tudor City Park in the south-west, the first of which has an observatory and planetarium. Also to the south are a 14th-century moated castle at Tillegem and a feudal farm, the Zeven Torentjes (Seven Towers). Further afield (but accessible by rail or bus tour) is the rebuilt town of Ieper (Ypres), once a flourishing medieval cloth town but best known as the centre of Flanders Fields during World War I.

See Atlas pages 138 – 139

Above: attractive whitewashed buildings in Lissewege.

Damme and Lissewege

Damme ① is accessible from Bruges via bus, paddle-steamer (the *Lamme Goedzak* moors at Noorweegse Kaai near Dampoort) or bike on a 7km (4-mile) ride alongside the canal. This genteel village was once the sea-port of Bruges and quite a large town. It retains an air of medieval prosperity, with a 15th-century town hall, a hospital for the poor, Sint-Janshospitaal, and a partly ruined church, Onze-Lieve-

Vrouwekerk (Church of Our Lady), built in 1340 over a chapel dating from 1225.

The village has made much of its literary connections. In front of the Town Hall stands a statue of the scholar-poet Jacob van Maerlant (1230–96), the 'father of Dutch poetry', who lived in Damme from around 1270, writing his most important works there. It has also adopted 14th-century German folk-tale character Tijl Uilenspiegel, who fetched up

in Damme by a circuitous route. The town has tried to reinvent itself as a book village modelled on Hay-on-Wye in Wales, but most visitors come for the restaurants, especially at weekends.

Lissewege ② is one of the best-preserved rural communities on the Flemish coastal plain; its pretty whitewashed houses have long been a draw for artists. A narrow canal, the Lisseweegs Vaartje, used to connect it with Bruges. The village is clustered around its early Gothic Onze-Lieve-Vrouwekerk (Church of Our Lady) (1225–50). Just outside the village used to stand the large Ter Doest abbey. Now only its vast tithe barn (1250) remains,

Left: discovering Damme by paddle-steamer.

moated castle surrounded by a 105-hectare (260-acre) country estate, the **Tillegembos**. In the eastern suburbs, in Assebroek, the **Zeven Torentjes** (Seven Towers) is a feudal manor farm that has been turned into a model farm, with animals and blacksmithing demonstrations.
SEE ALSO CHILDREN, P.44, 45; PARKS AND GARDENS, P.107

Ieper ③

A visit to Ieper (Ypres), south west of Bruges near the border with France, requires a full day. Coach tours are available from Bruges, or you can travel by train (1¾ hrs via Kortrijk), but you will need private transport to visit the cemeteries on the former battlefields.

One of the largest towns in Europe in the 13th century, with 40,000 inhabitants, Ieper was shelled to destruction during World War I, then reconstructed over the next 40 years. In the cloth hall on the Grote Markt, the powerful **In Flanders Fields Museum** uses historical documents, film footage, poetry, song and sounds to evoke the brutal experience of trench warfare in the Ypres Salient.

A short walk away is the **Menin Gate**, a memorial inscribed with the names of 55,000 of the 100,000 Commonwealth soldiers who died in battle but have no known grave. **Hill 62** remembers Canadian soldiers; at nearby **Sanctuary Wood Cemetery,** a few trenches are preserved; **Hill 60** commemorates the Australian dead. **Tyne Cot Military Cemetery** near Passendale has 12,000 graves. The German wardead are remembered in **Langemark** and **Vladslo**.

Tales of Tijl Uilenspiegel's adventures first appeared around 1480, in German prose tales. Damme, his 'birthplace', acquired him as a freedom fighter in Charles de Coster's epic novel *The Legend of the Glorious Adventures of Till Eulenspiegel* (1867; English 1918), which achieved international renown. In this version, the hero symbolises Flanders in its struggle against Spanish occupation.

attached to the manor farm, which is now a popular country inn, the Hof ter Doest.

Parks and Castles

There are many good options within 10km (6 mile) of Bruges to have a bracing walk and allow the kids to let off steam. The two large country estates of Beisbroek and Tudor City Park are next to each other alongside the Brussels–Ostend motorway.

Beisbroek covers 80 hectares (200 acres), and has a nature centre, planetarium and observatory; **Tudor City Park** covers 40 hectares (100 acres) and has a botanical garden, beehives and a castle (now a conference centre). The **Boudewijnpark** is a theme park with dolphinarium. South-west of Bruges, **Kasteel Tillegem** (Tillegem Castle) is a 14th-century

Below: remembering the dead of the Great War.

17

Ghent

The prosperous capital of the province of East Flanders, situated at the confluence of the Leie and Scheldt rivers, Ghent – Gent in Dutch – is a larger city than Bruges (population 235,000, of which 50,000 are students), with a younger vibe and a rich cultural life. It may not have such an unspoiled appearance, but its historic centre is well-preserved, with winding canals, cobbled streets and old buildings. Ghent was also seat of the Counts of Flanders and of their successors, the dukes of Burgundy, and flourished thanks to the cloth trade. Today, its port is the country's third largest, after Antwerp and Zeebrugge, connected to the sea by a canal.

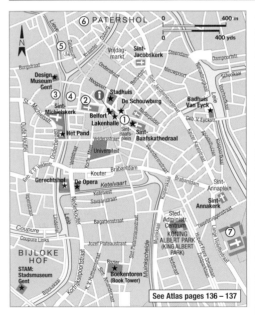

See Atlas pages 136 – 137

Together with the Belfort, the adjacent **Lakenhalle** (Cloth Hall) expresses Ghent's civic pride and wealth. The building, much restored, dates from 1441.

Across the road from the Lakenhalle in Botermarkt is the **Stadhuis** (Town Hall), built over several centuries starting in the early 16th.

Sint-Niklaaskerk

On the other side of the Belfort (Korenmarkt), **Sint-Niklaaskerk** ② (St Nicholas Church), built in the 13th-15th century, was the earliest of Ghent's three great towers

Below: Ghent has a younger vibe and lots of students.

Sint-Baafsplein ①

The largely Gothic brick and granite **Sint-Baafskathedraal** was built over several centuries: the chancel dates from the turn of the 14th century.

The tourist office in Ghent is located in the cellar of the Lakenhalle on Sint-Baafsplein, tel: 09 266 56 60, www.visitgent.be.

The cathedral's (and possibly the nation's) greatest treasure is The Adoration of the Mystic Lamb (1432), a 20-panel polyptych altarpiece regarded as the crowning achievement of Jan van Eyck's Gothic style and worth the trip to Ghent on its own.

Opposite the cathedral, the **Belfort** (Belfry), completed in 1380, has a 91m (298ft) tower with a lift.

Left: gaze at the view on Sint-Michielsbrug over the Leie.

For 10 days in mid-July, the city is given over to the annual Gentse Feesten (Ghent Festivities), a vast street festival centred around Bij Sint-Jacobs, Vlasmarkt and Sint-Jacobskerk (St James's Church). Part of the proceedings re-enacts the Stroppendragers (Noose Bearers) Procession, recalling Emperor Charles V's humiliation of the rebellious citizenry in 1540. For information, see www.gentsefeesten.be.

Patershol ⑥

A former working-class neighbourhood with narrow cobbled streets and quaint terraced houses, the Patershol district has been refurbished in recent years to become a lively restaurant quarter, buzzing with life by night. The nearby **Huis van Alijn** folklore museum offers a fantastic snapshot of daily life in Ghent over the centuries.

Vrijdagmarkt

The people of Ghent – *Gentenaars* – have risen up more than most in Flanders. They mainly gathered on Vrijdagmarkt, the city's main square, bordered by guild-houses and mansions, now cafés. A Friday market has been held here since the 13th century.

Small Begijnhof

Along Lange Violettenstraat, near Koning Albertpark (King Albert Park) is the tranquil **Klein Begijnhof** ⑦ (Small Begijnhof) or Onze-Lieve-Vrouw Ter Hoye (Our Lady of Hoye). Today it looks like a miniature walled 17th-century town, and is one of the finest surviving examples in the Low Countries.

SEE ALSO BEGUINAGES, P.28

(the others are the Belfort and Sint-Baafskathedraal).

Korenlei and Graslei

The two banks of the river Leie north of Sint-Michielsbrug are lined with medieval guild-houses. Korenlei ③, on the left, and Graslei ④, on the right, comprise Ghent's oldest harbour, the **Tussen Bruggen** (Between the Bridges), the commercial heart of the medieval city. At Korenlei 7 is the 1739 **Gildehuis van de Onvrije Schippers** (House of the Tied Boatmen), while at number 9 is the 16th-century **De Zwane** (The Swan), a former brewery. Across on Graslei is the **Gildehuis van de Vrije Schippers** (House of the Free Boatmen), built 1531 in Brabant Gothic style. Next door, the baroque **Gildehuis van de Graanmeters** (House of the Grain Weighers) dates from 1698.

There is a small **Tolhuisje** (Customs House), built in 1682, with the Romanesque-style **Het Spijker,** also known as Koornstapelhuis (a former grain warehouse dating from about 1200) next door. On the other side is the **Korenmetershuis** (Corn Measurer's house), followed by the Gothic-style **Gildehuis van de Metselaars** (House of the Masons), built 1912 according to plans of the original.

Gravensteen ⑤

This heavily renovated island fortress was once the Castle of the Counts. Work began on the structure in 1180, on the site of a 9th-century castle and modelled on the Crusader castles of the Holy Land. The battlements and keep can be visited; the latter includes the Great Hall where the Knights of the Golden Fleece were feted in 1445.

19

The Coast

Just 15km (9 miles) from Bruges is the North Sea coast and Belgium's short stretch of coastline, dotted with resorts and dunes. Access to the coast is easy with the coastal tram, which runs from the Dutch border to the French, often just metres behind the dunes. Its journey takes in ritzy Knokke-Heist; the seaport of Zeebrugge; the yacht harbour at Blankenberge; the beach and dunes of Wenduine; the *belle-époque* glory of De Haan; popular Ostend; the fishing harbour of Nieuwpoort; the seafood restaurants of Oostduinkerke; and the beaches of Koksijde and De Panne, where sand-yachts sail in the wind. Three resorts are described below.

Zeebrugge ①

The nearest coastal town to Bruges is Zeebrugge, literally 'Sea-Bruges', a port-town created by King Leopold II (1835–1909) in 1904, and joined to it by a 12km (7½-mile) canal – the Boudewijnkanaal. The port was destroyed in both World Wars, but Zeebrugge rose again to become Belgium's largest fishing port, as well as a major container-ship and ferry port. The main attraction is a maritime theme park in the former fish market: **Seafront Zeebrugge.**

SEE ALSO CHILDREN, P.45

De Haan ②

Another King Leopold II project, designed as a bathing resort, De Haan has a genteel charm. Reached from Bruges by a train to Ostend and then the tram towards Knokke, the town is named after the first hotel that opened here, in 1888: **De Haan Hotel** (The Rooster Hotel). Shortly after,

the king instructed two architects to build a beach town. The result was a series of individual villas in *belle-époque* style. Strict rules determined the planting of green areas and the height of buildings. The rules still apply and the district, known as the Concession, lends De Haan its character. The **tram shelter** dates from 1902 and is in art nouveau style; it also

houses the tourist office. Belgium's first golf course, the 18-hole **Royal Golf Club**, opened here in 1903, and Albert Einstein lived here for six months in 1933. Two typical hotels are the **Grand-Hôtel Belle-Vue**, which opened in the 1920s, and the **Hôtel des Brasseurs**, which dates from 1900. The country-style villas at **Rembrandt-laan 10–19** date from

Below: De Haan's tourist office is in this former tram shelter.

Left: young readers browsing at the beach library.

The British frequented Ostend en masse during its 19th-century heyday, arriving in ferries from Dover to play lawn tennis, golf and beach croquet. In the 1860s, there were 2,000 British residents out of the town's population of 16,000.

Zee, Art Museum by the Sea), where the collection also includes works by René Magritte, Constant Permeke, Leon Spilliaert, Pierre Alechinsky and Panamarenko, shown on rotation. It also hosts temporary shows by contemporary artists.

Visserskaai is lined with fish stalls and restaurants serving whelk soup, Ostend sole, oysters and mussels. Fishing boats draw up here and sell their catch to restaurateurs. Set into the quay, the Amandine is a former Icelandic trawler that makes for a good visit. The highlight of the marina round the corner is the three-masted former Belgian Navy training yacht, the *Mercator*.

SEE ALSO PAINTING AND SCULPTURE, P.96

Below: colourful boats at Ostend marina.

Soul legend Marvin Gaye lived in Ostend for two years, and wrote his 1982 hit *Sexual Healing* there, in self-imposed exile from a life of drug and alcohol abuse. Shortly afterwards, he returned to Los Angeles where, aged 44, he was shot dead by his father.

1925–7. De Haan has an active sailing and windsurfing club, **Watersportclub De Windhaan**, which rents out catamarans and teaches kitesurfing. Behind the long sandy beach are several nature reserves, including **Natuurreservaat De Kijkuit**, with sand-fixing vegetation to prevent coastal erosion.

Ostend ③

There are three trains an hour from Bruges to Belgium's largest seaside resort, which in the 19th century tried to rival the grand French resorts of Deauville and Biarritz. The Belgian royal family kept a villa here until 2005, and wealthy foreigners stayed here including Russian tsars and Britain's Queen Victoria, who attended the **English church**. The **Casino Kursaal** was rebuilt in 1953, and recently reopened as a convention and concert venue, with a fish restaurant on the top floor. At the other end of the promenade is the **Thermae Palace Hotel**, a 1930s former spa, now a hotel. It stands above the 400m (1,300ft) of **royal arcades**, a colonnaded walkway built in 1905 to link the royal villa to the racecourse. Painter James Ensor (1860–1949), whose work opened the way for Surrealism and Expressionism, lived and worked in Ostend: his former house, the **James Ensorhuis** is now a museum including his studio. Original artworks by Ensor can be seen at the decent **MuZee** (Kunstmuseum aan

21

A–Z

In the following section Bruges's attractions and services are organised by theme, under alphabetical headings. Items that link to another theme are cross-referenced. All sights that are plotted on the atlas section at the end of the book are given a page number and grid reference.

Architecture

Long agreed to be one of the most beautiful cities in Europe, Bruges' architectural wealth gained official recognition when Unesco designated the historic centre a World Heritage site in 2000. The city was instrumental in developing the brick Gothic style from the 13th century, but after the neo-Gothic restoration of the old centre in the 19th century, there was scant enthusiasm for subsequent movements. The recent economic revival in Flanders, however, has kickstarted enthusiasm for new, bolder projects. This section highlights buildings that have made significant architectural contributions to Bruges.

Concertgebouw

't Zand 34; tel: 050 47 69 99; www.concertgebouw.be; guided visits by arrangement only; bus: 0/Centrum; map p.134 B3

A striking example of contemporary architecture in a city that thrives on the past, the vast concert hall designed by Paul Robberecht and Hilde Daem to mark the city's year as European Capital of Culture in 2002, is clad in 68,000 terracotta tiles, a nod to the red-brick of medieval Bruges. The taller part of the structure, known as the 'lantern tower', twinkles at night through dozens of tiny windows overlooking the square. Inside, the space is minimalist, with bare concrete walls and columns. The Kamermuziekzaal (chamber music hall) is highly original: the audience sits in single rows in bays arranged vertically around the stage.
SEE ALSO MUSIC, P.92

Heilig Bloedbasiliek

Burg 15; tel: 050 33 67 92; www.holyblood.com; Basilica: Apr–Sept 9.30am–noon, 2–6pm, Oct–Mar 10am–noon, 2–4pm; free; bus: 0/Centrum; map p.134 C4

Behind the intricate Renaissance facade of the Basilica of the Holy Blood is the Romanesque lower chapel (1139), one of the few local examples of the style said to copy that used during Roman times. The heavy cylindrical columns, semicircular arches, small windows and thick stone walls are characteristic of the style. The late 15th-century upper chapel was remodelled in the late 18th century: the pulpit dates from 1728; the stained glass windows from 1845.
SEE ALSO CHURCHES, P.46; MUSEUMS AND GALLERIES, P.82

Onze-Lieve-Vrouwekerk

Mariastraat; tel: 050 44 87 11; www.brugge.be/musea; Mon–Sat 9.30am–4.50pm, Sun 1.30–4.50pm; free; bus: 1; map p.134 C3

Below: the decorative facade of Oude Griffie.

Many of the domestic buildings in Bruges have step gables, which also feature in many cityscapes by the Flemish Primitives. The step form offered a type of fire protection for urban houses: the gable extension would slow the spread of sparks from one roof to another. The steps also provided convenient access to the roof for chimney sweeps and roofers in times when cranes were non-existent and tall ladders uncommon. Fine examples are at Jan Van Eyckplein and, in more modest form, in the old tradesmen's houses facing the Belfry on the Markt.

Left: orange tiles and stepped gables on Bruges rooftops.

vated with a colourful, authentic, polychrome facade. The bas-relief depicts the ancient Persian legend of a king having a corrupt judge skinned alive (see Gerard David's 1498 painting on the same gruesome theme in the Groeningemuseum, *p.85*), a popular cautionary tale for lawmakers in medieval times. Today the building is occupied by the law courts and is not open to the public.

Paleis van het Brugse Vrije

Burg 11a; tel: 050 44 87 11; www.brugge.be/musea; daily 9.30am–12.30pm, 1.30–5pm; entrance charge; bus: 0/Centrum; map 135 C4

Although at its heart is a much older building, the visible face of the Brugse Vrije is typical of the neoclassical architectural fashion of the 18th century, adopting a more restrained form of classical architecture than the

The dominant spire of the Church of Our Lady is characteristic of the austere, Scaldian (river Scheldt) Gothic style, which developed in the early 13th century. The movement was characterised by its solid aspect, and double or triple lancet windows. Built out of brick, the 122m (400ft) spire is the city's tallest landmark.
SEE ALSO CHURCHES, P.47

Oude Griffie

Burg 11a; closed to public; bus: 0/Centrum; map p.135 C4

Built 1534–7, the ornate Oude Griffie (Old Recorder's House), or Civic Registry, is an example of Flemish Renaissance, adapted from the Italian style to suit the practical needs and stylistic sensibilities of the Low Countries, and recently reno-

Below: the Concertgebouw is a rare example of contemporary architecture in Bruges.

preceding baroque period. It was not widely adopted in Flanders, where many Catholics rejected what they saw as an aping of styles developed by ancient pagan cultures. They were happy to embrace the neo-Gothic revival which followed soon after. The buildings around the courtyard are mainly city council offices, but they also give access to the fine Renaissancezaal.

SEE ALSO MUSEUMS AND GALLERIES, P.82

't Pandreitje

Pand 7; bus: 1, 11; map p.134 C3

A modern housing complex begun in 2000 on the site of a former prison alongside Koningin Astridpark. The small 'garden city' was the result of a competition held to provide family homes close to the city centre. The car-free estate is composed of 75 urban dwellings with underground parking, made of brick and with small walled gardens or terraces sympa-

thetic to the city's medieval housing style. The complex was completed in 2002.

Paviljoen Toyo Ito

Burg; bus: 0/Centrum; map p.135 C4

The honeycomb steel-and-glass pavilion on the Burg was commissioned from leading Japanese architect Toyo Ito, like the Concertgebouw, for Bruges' year as European Capital of Culture in 2002. Originally intended as a temporary structure, the walkway was designed to symbolise the connection between the Bruges of yesterday and today: the circle of gravel (which has replaced the original watery surround) marks the site of the altar of the city's former cathedral, St Donatian's, whose footings and ruins can be seen in the basement of the Crowne Plaza hotel. Locally, the pavilion is known as the 'Governor's Carwash' (the provincial governor's palace lies next door, to the west).

Provinicaal Hof

Markt 3; not open to public; bus: 0/Centrum; map p.134 C4

The former provincial government building, built 1881–1921, is a proud example of the neo-Gothic style, which found such favour in Bruges. Bruges-born architect Louis Delacenserie (1838–1909) designed the palatial structure, and was behind the restoration of many other medieval buildings in the city. The red-brick building to the right is the main post office, on the site of the old medieval cloth hall, which spanned the canal that passed under the building. Delacenserie also designed Antwerp's grandiose Centraal Station.

Sint-Walburgakerk

St Maartensplein; daily 10am–noon, 2–5pm, Sun pm only; free; bus: 6, 16; map p.133 C1

This elegant church is a rare example in Bruges of pure baroque architecture, designed by Jesuit priest Pieter Huyssens and built

Below: the stately facade of the Provinicaal Hof.

Art nouveau, the 'new art' style adopted by architects across Europe in the 19th century in a bid to break free of derivative forms such as neo-Gothic, made an enormous impact in Brussels but largely passed by Bruges. Just three examples can be seen in the city: the shopfront of De Medici Sorbetière at 9 Geldmuntstraat; a pair of house facades behind the Onze-Lieve-Vrouwekerk (6-8 Onze-Lieve-Vrouwekerk-Zuid), built in 1904, with murals depicting Day and Night painted over the doorways; and the facade of Pietje Pek bistro at 13 Sint-Jakobsstraat.

1619–41. Exemplifying the renewed confidence of Catholicism and the Counter-Reformation after the religious strife of the 16th century, it has all the rich embellishment for which the style is known: garlands, swirls, barley-sugar twists, broken pediments, oval windows and cherubs. The light interior features black-and-white marble floor tiles and white columns. Baroque features can also be observed inside many other Bruges churches (Sint-Anna, for example), although their external structures mainly date from earlier periods. Exuberant carved pulpits by the likes of Artus Quellinus the Younger and Hendrik Verbruggen are typical of the style.

SEE ALSO CHURCHES, P.50

Stadhuis

Burg 12; tel: 050 44 87 11; www.brugge.bc/museca; daily 9.30am–5pm; entrance charge; bus: 0/Centrum; map p.135 C4

The late 14th century saw the emergence of Flamboyant Gothic, adopted for secular use such as for this, the oldest town hall in the Low Countries, built 1376–1421. The style can be recognised for its delicate window tracery, spires, finials and sculpture. The building became the model for several city halls in Belgium, most notably those in Leuven, Brussels and Oudenaarde. The facade would originally have been brightly painted.

Beneath the windows are the coats of arms of towns that came under the jurisdiction of Bruges until 1795; they are not all correct because their design was based on an inaccurate document. The 34 figures of saints, prophets and noblemen and women that decorate the niches are copies of the originals, which were removed by the Jacobins and their Flemish sympathisers, then destroyed on the Markt. They represent 34 important figures in the history of Flanders.

On the top of the twisted chimney stacks sit gold crowns, a gift from the king of France, who so admired the wise aldermen of Bruges that he wanted to crown their breath as it left the chamber.

The fantastic Gothic Hall on the first floor is the only area open to the public.

SEE ALSO MONUMENTS, P.81

Below: the light and cool interior of Sint-Walburgakerk.

Beguinages

Flanders is famous for the number of its surviving enclosed residences for Beguines, unmarried or widowed women who adopted a life of religious devotion but without taking the full vows of a nun. The Beguinage of Bruges is a well-preserved example of this form of residence, and is one of the best loved and most photographed sights in the city. A wander through its walled garden-courtyard, with swishing poplars and cooing doves, is like a trip back in time to another age. This chapter explains the origin and the life of these unique, fascinating communities.

Origin

Beguines were initially solitary women who worked helping the poor and preaching. Progressively, and in the face of a growing suspicion on the part of male religious authorities, they grouped together to live in a walled residential community known as a Beguinage (French) or Begijnhof (Dutch). The first Beguinage in Belgium appeared in Mechelen in 1207.

Beguinages were formed across the southern Netherlands from the 12th century onwards. Of the 100 that existed in the 14th century, around 25 remain. In 1998, 13 surviving Flemish Beguinages were placed on the Unesco World Heritage list. They are located in the following towns: Hoogstraten, Lier, Mechelen, Turnhout, Sint-Truiden, Tongeren, Dendermonde, Ghent (2), Diest, Leuven, Bruges and Kortrijk. Most of their buildings date from the 17th century. In their original, medieval form, the houses would have been wooden constructions.

Above: the Begijnhof entrance can be seen from the water.

Beguines

Beguines lived in solitude in separate small houses. They divided their time between prayer, manual work (sewing or lace-making) and taking part in collective Beguinage events, such as religious services and processions. Some Beguinages selected their members on the basis of social status; others were open to all, and numbered their inhabitants in thousands.

Beguines have been described as the earliest women's movement in Christian history, a community of financially independent women who existed outside the church and the home, the only acceptable domains for women at the time.

The male counterparts of Beguines were known as

Left: a nun crosses the Begijnhof courtyard.

most were quashed following the French Revolution and they became extinct in the early 20th century.

Current Inhabitants

The Beguinage in Bruges is today occupied in part by a community of Benedictine nuns, who wear the traditional clothes of the Beguines and maintain some of their predecessors' customs. Other houses are occupied by lay people. The Beguinage in Leuven is inhabited by university students and lecturers. Elsewhere, they are occupied by retired people or cultural institutions.

The Bruges Beguinage

Prinselijk Begijnhof De Wijngaarde

Wijngaardplein; daily 6.30am–6.30pm; free; bus: 1; map p.134 B2

The Prinselijk Begijnhof De Wijngaard was founded in 1245. At its height, in the 17th century, it numbered up to 300 houses, stretching as far as today's railway station, and was a self-governing community, with a hospice, farm and brewery, as well as a church. Carved bunches of grapes on the bridge handrail and over the doorway by the entrance (1776) recall its earlier surroundings: a vineyard where grapes were cultivated for vinegar-making, hence the name: Princely Beguinage of the Vineyard. The word 'sauvegarde' above the door attests to the royal protection granted by the Duke of Burgundy, assuring the Beguinage's independent status. The last Beguines left in 1927.

SEE ALSO CHURCHES, P.47;
MUSEUMS AND GALLERIES, P.84

At their origin in the 12th century, Beguinages were usually built on the edge of a city, and became a tiny town within a town, situated near water that the residents could use for their textile work and vegetable plots. Later, with the wars of religion, the area surrounded by the city walls was extended, and encapsulated the Beguinage. Interest in preserving Beguinages grew from the mid-19th century, when artists started to depict the folkloric charm of these uniquely preserved, miniature towns.

leave without permission from their superior. The enclosures also became centres of mysticism, their members practising flagellation and other activities considered heretical. In 1311, Pope Clement V accused Beguines of spreading heresy; they were persecuted by the Church for many years, until rehabilitated in the 15th century. In Belgium, the Beguinages flourished under Spanish rule, especially from the 17th century on. However,

Below: a detail from the gate to the Begijnhof.

Begharads, and were usually of humble origin. Similar to Beguines in that they were not bound by vows and did not follow a uniform rule of life, they differed in the that they had no private property, lived together in a cloister and ate at the same table.

Decline

Over time, Beguinages grew to resemble monastic orders: Beguines had to follow strict rules and were not allowed to

Cafés and Bars

There are few greater pleasures in Bruges than reflecting on the historical treasures around you while sitting in a bar or café sipping a Belgian beer. You will be spoilt for choice: most bars stock at least 20 beer varieties; a few have more than 100. Or how about a coffee and *pannekoeken* (pancakes) for a spot of people-watching after a museum? Many bars and cafés stay open until the early hours of the morning, until the last customers leave. For a guide to Belgian beers, *see 'Food and Drink'*. For bars that have live music or DJ sets, *see 'Nightlife'*. Many bars and cafés listed here will serve food, but *see also 'Restaurants'*.

Markt and Burg

Cambrinus
Philipstockstraat 19; tel: 050 33 23 28; www.cambrinus.eu; daily 11am–11pm, later at weekends; bus: 0/Centrum; map p.134 C4
Under the same ownership as the nearby De Bier Tempel store and with rather a tourist focus, this newish bar-brasserie has similar expertise in the hallowed hop: 400 beers are on offer in a renovated pub-like decor with coloured glass lamps, a long bar and table service. Good portions of hearty food – including some recipes cooked with beer – complete the experience and ensure that if you spend enough time in here, you could end up looking like the rotund chap straddling a beer barrel in the

Above: Cambrinus's rotund logo, a warning to all beer drinkers...

establishment's logo. That will be Cambrinus, the 'king of beer'. You have been warned.

Charlie Rockets
Hoogstraat 19; tel: 050 33 06 60; www.charlierockets.com; daily 8am–4am; bus: 0/Centrum, 6, 16; map p.135 C4
A young, alternative clientele comes to this American-style bar-diner that stays open late into the night (be warned anyone considering staying in the youth hostel upstairs). It is on two floors, located in a former cinema that is still intact. There are also five pool tables, darts and a resident DJ at weekends.

Craenenburg
Markt 16; tel: 050 33 34 02; www.craenenburg.be; Mon–Tue, Thur–Sat from 7.30am, Wed from 7am, Sun from 8am, until 10–11pm in winter, 1–2am summer; bus: 0/Centrum; map p.134 C4
Probably the best-known café in Bruges, due to its location and history: it was here that Margaret of York stood to watch jousting tournaments in honour of her marriage to Charles the Bold in 1468. Twenty years later, Archduke

Smoking is permitted in Belgian bars and cafés except those where food is served, in which case there must be a designated non-smoking area. The non-smoking area can, in certain establishments, be more notional than real, due to the lack of any physical barrier.

Left: packed café terraces on a sunny day.

spreads and tarts, and generous breakfasts, but the tasty open sandwiches are not for larger appetites.

Staminée de Garre
De Garre 1; tel: 050 34 10 29; Mon–Thur noon–midnight, Fri noon–1am, Sat 11am–1am, Sun 11am–midnight; bus: 0/Centrum; map p.134 C4

A place of pilgrimage for beer-lovers, many of whom struggle to find the narrow alley De Garre – more a door in the wall off Breidelstraat – or cannot get a seat once in (and standing is not allowed). On two floors of an old house with no smoking upstairs (though be warned the serving staff may forget you are up there), it is a friendly place where the 130 beers on offer come served with cheese. House brew Tripel de Garre (11.5 percent) is a must-try; it is limited to three glasses per person.

Wijnbar Est
Braambergstraat 7; tel: 050 33 38 39; www.wijnbarest.be; Mon, Thur–Fri, Sun from 2pm, Sat from noon; bus: 6, 16; map p.135 C4

Attractive, tiny wine bar on

Hot drinks are usually served with a sweet biscuit, piece of chocolate or small cake; beers come with savoury nibbles. If you prefer a milky coffee, ask for a *'koffie verkeerd'*, which is made with more hot milk than coffee. This is not to be confused with cappuccino, which in Belgium is usually made with a dollop of whipped cream on a black coffee and not frothy milk, as you find in Italy (and most other places). Tea served in Belgium is generally disappointing, especially if you like a strong brew. It invariably comes served as a cup of hot (not boiling) water with a flavourless bag on the side.

Het Dagelijks Brood
Philipstockstraat 21; tel: 050 33 60 50; www.painquotidien.com; daily 8am–6pm; bus: 0/Centrum; map p.134 C4

Local branch of hit Belgian bakery and café (known as Le Pain Quotidien in French-speaking parts), which has franchised its scrubbed-pine communal table philosophy to cities around the world. Wholesome bread, dangerously addictive chocolate

---

Maximilian of Austria was held hostage here by locals furious at his attempt to impose taxes on them; his advisers were tortured here, too. A traditional Flemish café, it has been run by the same family since the 1960s. Good terrace for people-watching, and for breakfast, as the sunlight falls here in the morning. Varied brasserie fare.

Below: the historic Craenenburg café.

two floors run by a welcoming and knowledgeable family. Daily menu of wines by the glass, plus 90 more by the bottle. Platters of cheese and charcuterie plus salads and pasta enhance the tasting experience, and there are live concerts of jazz, blues, boogie, folk or pop every Sunday from 8–10.30pm; free entry.

South

De Bühne

Sint-Salvatorskoorstraat 6; tel: 050 34 66 49; Wed–Mon noon–9pm; bus: 0/Centrum, 1; map p.134 B3

Inviting tea room and lunch spot off Simon Stevinplein that does divine pastries, for a break away from the crowds and no risk of soggy pancakes.

Carpe Diem

Wijngaardstraat 8; tel: 050 33 54 47; www.tearoom-carpediem.be; Wed–Mon 7am–6.30pm, bakery until 7pm; bus: 1; map p.134 C2

Wood-panelling, antiques and stained-glass doors make the perfect accompaniments to an 'olde-worlde' experience in the tearoom adjoining the Detavernier patisserie and bakery. Run by a dynamic couple, it is quiet and civilized without being over-smart. Mouthwatering cakes and biscuits.

L'Estaminet

Park 5; tel: 050 33 09 16; Tue, Wed, Fri–Sun 11.30am–late, Thur 4pm–late; bus: 1, 11; map p.135 D3

Open since 1900, this family-friendly café gets packed with locals on a Sunday afternoon, after the obligatory stroll round the Astridpark just across the road. A jolly, laid-back establishment, which

Two beers are still brewed in Bruges: Straffe Hendrik and Brugse Zot, both made by the Halve Maan Brewery. Try them unfiltered exclusively in the brewery's bar. Halve Maan had transferred production of Straffe Hendrik to another brewery in 1988, but brought it back in-house in 2008, restoring to the city its only 'Tripel'. A number of other Belgian beers are named after Bruges: Brugge Blond, Brugge Tripel, Brugs, Brugs Tarwebier and Brugse Babbelaar.

serves tasty spaghetti Bolognese and other simple bar meals, plays the blues and sometimes hosts live music.

De Halve Maan

Walplein 26; tel: 050 33 26 97; www.halvemaan.be; daily 10am–6pm; bus: 1; map p.134 C2

The sole working brewery in Bruges, run by one family since 1856, and a brewery museum as well as a bar. Records from 1564 also note the existence on Walplein of a brewery called Die Maene (The Moon). Its two house beers are Straffe Hendrik (Strong Henry) – recently repurchased after it was sold to another producer – and Brugse Zot (Bruges Fool), created in 2005. A vast range of other brews are served in the roomy and family-friendly tavern, as well as an affordable dish-of-the-day. The sunny courtyard gets busy in fine weather. Tours are on the hour from 11am–4pm (5pm on Sat) in Apr–Oct; at 11am and 3pm (Sat–Sun hourly 11am–4pm) in Nov–Mar.

West

De Belegde Boterham

Kleine Sint-Amandsstraat 5; tel: 050 34 91 31; Mon–Sat noon–4pm; bus: 0/Centrum; map p.134 B4

Below: the sign for De Halve Maan brewery.

Above: if you like beer, 't Brugs Beertje is the place for you...

A fresh and funky small sandwich bar and tea room on a little pedestrianised street near the Markt, serving tasty salads, sandwiches and light lunches.

't Brugs Beertje
Kemelstraat 5; tel: 050 33 96 16; www.brugsbeertje.be; Thur–Tue 4pm–1am, Sat–Sun until 2am; bus: 0/Centrum; map p.134 B3

The beer connoisseur's favourite bar in Bruges, as small inside as its reputation is large, this has become a beer-lovers mecca since it was established some 20 years ago. The friendly and knowledgeable landlord will advise on all aspects of his 300 or so beers. Snacks and light meals are served, and

there is a shop where you can buy the T-shirt.

Concertgebouwcafé
't Zand 34; tel: 050 47 69 99; www.concertgebouw.be; Wed–Sat 11am–late plus on performance days from 1hr before show; bus: 0/Centrum; p.134 B3

The new concert hall café – located between the tourist office and the hall's main entrance – is as minimalist and stylish as the rest of the building. A light food menu and varied wine list is complemented by refined music on the sound system and a no-smoking policy. Happy hour every Friday from 5–6pm (two drinks for the price of one).

De Medici Sorbetière
9 Geldmuntstraat; tel: 050 33 93 41; www.demedici.be; all year Mon–Tue, Thur–Sat 9am–6pm, Apr–mid-Oct also Wed noon–6pm, mid-Oct–Mar also Sun 3–6pm; bus: 0/Centrum; map p.134 B4

An ice-cream parlour and tea-room that upholds the Burgundian traditions of fine

Below: ... and it is a cosy spot to pause and catch up.

Cocktails

Mojito
Mojito Royal
Caipirinha
Caipiroska
Margarita
Daiquiri

Pina Colada
Nutty Colada
White Russian
Black Russian
Long Island
Iced tea
Mai Tai

Tequila Sunrise
Tequila Steeler
Harvey Wallbanger
Singapore Sling
Bee's Knees

Above: the Wereldcafé De Republiek has an extensive cocktail menu...

feasting in a pretty art deco interior on two floors with a terrace on the first floor to the rear. Also does some seriously wicked cakes.

North

't Opkikkertje

West-Gistelhof 13; tel: 0485 94 94 83; www.opkikkertje.be; Mon–Tue, Thur–Fri from 4.30pm, Wed from 6pm, Sat from 5pm; bus: 4, 14; map p.132 C2

Mingle with local workers and

Below: try something fruity...

bohemians at this tucked away and very local bar, which serves the cheapest beers in town during its daily happy hour, 5–6pm (except Wed when the happy hour is for genever, the local gin).

Patisserie Servaas van Mullem

Vlamingstraat 56; tel: 050 33 05 15; Wed–Mon 7.30am–6pm; bus: 0/Centrum, 3, 13; map p.132 C1

Well-dressed professionals and academic types take their morning coffee over a paper at this upmarket bakery and pastry shop with a tempting spread of cakes and fruit tarts. There is a small terrace alongside the shop, facing the theatre.

Poatersgat

Vlamingstraat 82; www. poatersgat.com; daily 5pm–late;

Table service is standard in all bars and cafés but the most hip – a trend that we hope does not catch on. You are not expected to tip the staff, but they will appreciate if you leave a few coins to round up the bill, especially if you are in a group.

bus: 3, 13; map p.132 C1

Atmospheric beer pub (120 brews on the menu) in a stunning vaulted cellar, prettily candlelit and popular with a local, younger crowd late in the evening. The name means 'monk's hole' in the local dialect, a reference to the below-ground entrance from the street.

Prestige

Vlamingstraat 12–14; tel: 050 34 31 67; Mon–Sat 7.30am–6pm,

Below: ...or cool and refreshing.

Above: Vino Vino is a popular tapas and live music bar.

Sun 8am–5pm; bus: 0/Centrum; map p.132 C1

Chintzy, luxurious tearoom alongside a good bakery and pastry shop just off the Markt. A recent makeover has seen prices escalate, but the decor is delightful and service welcoming, whether for breakfast, lunch or tea.

Terrastje
Genthof 45; tel: 050 33 09 19; Fri–Tue noon–midnight, Sept–May closed Tue from 4pm; bus: 4, 14; map p.133 C1

Cosy brown café in a tiny building with a slightly larger terrace, right on a road junction overlooking the canal. Run by a friendly English-Dutch couple and loved by locals and visitors alike, it is prized for its good beer selection, tasty brasserie fare (soup, snails, *waterzooi*, omelette, salads), wide selection of nibbles (ham and cheese platters) and desserts (ices and pan-cakes). Live jazz every first Mon of month from Dec–Sept.

Vino Vino
Grauwwerkersstraat 15; tel: 050 34 51 15; Tue–Sat 6pm–3am; bus: 3, 13; map p.132 B1

Jugs of sangria, portions of tapas, blues on the sound system and a friendly owner have earned this backstreet wine bar a faithful following.

Wereldcafé De Republiek
Sint-Jakobsstraat 36; tel: 050 34 02 29; www.derepubliek.be;

Below: sticky, sweet pancakes and waffles are a Belgian staple.

In addition to complementary peanuts or small nibbles, most bars in Belgium sell tempting 'mixed portions' for a few euros – either a plate of cheese chunks, or salami slices, or both, usually with celery salt, mustard and pickles on the side. Shared between 2–4 people, these make for a filling snack with a few beers.

Above: nibbles are often served with your drinks order.

daily 11am–2am (earliest); bus: 0/Centrum, 3, 13; map p.134 B4
Café of the Cultuurhuis de Republiek that includes the Lumière art-house cinema. Popular with a local, alternative crowd, it also serves cocktails and exotic light meals (up to 11pm, after which only a limited choice). Large courtyard behind is a real suntrap.

East

Barsalon
Langestraat 15; tel: 050 61 09 38; www.rock-fort.be; Mon–Fri noon–2.30pm, 6pm–midnight; bus: 6, 16; map p.135 D4
Trendy lounge bar-brasserie merged in a sliver of a place

with Rock Fort restaurant, whose dining area spills into the bar. Ideal for a tête-à-tête, the high tables have white leather-covered fixed stools.
SEE ALSO RESTAURANTS, P.119

Bauhaus
Langestraat 135–137; tel: 050 34 10 93; www.bauhaus.be; daily 8am–1am, Sat–Sun until 4am; bus: 6, 16; map p.133 E1
Laid-back café attached to the youth hostel and budget hotel; so populated by young people from all over the world, and plenty of locals, too. They come here for the cheap eats, large beer selection, monthly open mic night and the DJ on Fri and Sat. Spread across two rooms, with smoking permitted on the bar side.

Du Phare
Sasplein 2; tel: 050 34 35 90; www.duphare.be; Wed–Mon 11.30am–1am, Sat–Sun until 4am; food served: 11.30am–2.30pm, 7pm–midnight, Fri–Sat until 2am; bus: 4; map p.133 D4
Up near the Dampoort, this music bar-brasserie has a friendly atmosphere, varied menu (Creole, Thai, steaks) and live blues and jazz bands. A large south-facing terrace beside the canal is a draw. Busiest at night, but a pleasant spot for lunch or drinks when you are in this neck of the woods.

Below: friendly bar service at backpacker haven, Bauhaus.

55; www.dullegriet.be; Mon 4.30pm–1am, Tue–Sat noon–1am, Sun noon–7.30pm; tram: 1; map p.136 C4

There is no shortage of cafés on Vrijdagmarkt, but this is one of the highlights, an Old Flemish-style bar with 250 different beers, including the renowned Kwak – the 1.5-litre glasses are on proud display – and Ghent's own brews Stropken, Gentse Tripel and Augustijnerbier. Last orders half an hour before closing time.

't Dreupelkot

Groentenmarkt 12; tel: 09 224 21 20; www.waterhuisaan debierkant.be; daily 4pm–3am; tram: 1; map p.136 C4

Bruges no longer has a dedicated genever specialist but Ghent does, run by the same team as the Waterhuis aan de Bierkant. Step inside to sample this traditional Belgian tipple in all its varieties.

Kafee Vooruit

Sint-Pietersnieuwstraat 23; tel: 09 267 28 48; www.vooruit.be; Mon–Thur 11.30am–2am, Fri, Sat 11.30am–3am, Sun 4pm–1am; tram: 22; map p.137 C2

The restored Kunstcentrum Vooruit is a remarkable vision of a working-class culture palace dating from 1912. Its vast café is popular with students and bohemian types, and serves drinks, coffee and light veggie meals.

Het Waterhuis aan de Bierkant

Groentenmarkt 9; tel: 09 225 06 80; www.waterhuisaande bierkant.be; daily 11am–1am; tram: 1; map p.136 C4

A justifiably popular bar in a great location right beside the Leie; try Ghent's own beers Stropken, Gentse Tripel and Augustijnerbier, among the 150 on offer.

Vlissinghe

Blekersstraat 2; tel: 050 34 37 37; www.cafevlissinghe.be; Wed–Sat 11am–midnight, Sun 11am–7pm; bus: 4, 14; map p.133 D1

Founded in 1515, this is the oldest café in Bruges, with wood-panelled walls, long oak tables and a good-sized garden. The beer list is not that impressive and the bar food is simple, but this is an institution: come to relive the Bruges of yore. Open later than advertised on Fri and Sat, as long as the punters keep drinking.

Ghent

Brooderie

Jan Breydelstraat 8; tel: 09 225 06 23; www.brooderie.be; Tue–Sun 8am–6pm; tram: 1; map p.136 C4

Facing the Design Museum, this homely bakery store (with B&B rooms upstairs) serves breakfast, lunch and afternoon teas on scrubbed pine tables. Cakes are home-made and portions are generous: try the moist, dark spice cake.

De Dulle Griet

Vrijdagmarkt 50; tel: 09 224 24

37

Canals and Bridges

The canals – *reien* – of Bruges give the city its almost impossible prettiness. The red-brick architecture is duplicated in reflection to create picture-perfect views of a bygone age. But what delights us today once came with an ugly smell: sewage was dumped into the canals right up until 1980. A boat tour is an excellent way to view the city, but to best appreciate the canals, wander on foot or cycle around the following highlights, presented in alphabetical order by quayside, followed by bridges along that particular stretch of water.

Coupure

Bus: 6, 16; map p.135 D1–E3

The Coupure is a former industrial leg of canal, dug in 1752 to allow river traffic from Ghent a shorter route via the Sint-Annarei to the Langerei. It was an industrial neighbourhood until the start of World War II. Towards the southern end is a popular mooring spot for yachts and cabin cruisers, and for fishermen trying their luck from the quay. It feels quite rural compared to the rest of the city.

> The open-topped canal boats operate Mar–Nov daily 10am–6pm and at weekends and holiday periods through the winter, weather permitting. Boats depart from Rozenhoed-kaai, Dijver and Mariastraat.

Conzett Brug

Bus: 6, 16; map p.135 E3

This modern footbridge was designed by architect Jürg Conzett to mark Bruges' year as European Capital of Culture in 2002. Great scrolls of rusted steel span the canal above the walkway of weather-washed wood, which has proved very welcome to locals since it was built, providing the missing link in the ring canal park.

Dampoort

Bus: 4; map p.133 D4

The modern working canal, complete with lifting bridges, makes fun family viewing at Dampoort and the adjacent Handelskom Docks. These were dug in 1664–65 to take advantage of the new network of inland waterways passing through Bruges, and were once used by sea-going vessels. It is still busy with working barges as it is close to the start of the Boudewijnkanaal (Baudouin Canal) to Zeebrugge and the canal to Ostend which, from 1622 onwards, restored the city's link with the sea, lost after the route via Damme and the Zwin estuary inlet silted up.

Gouden-Handrei

Bus: 4, 14; map p.133 C1

The start of a tranquil stretch of canal branching off Langerei, providing welcome

Below: the Conzett Brug is one of the city's newest bridges.

Left: a boat passes under the Meebrug *(see p.40)*.

Swans have swum in Bruges' canals, so the story goes, since 1448, when Emperor Maximilian was imprisoned in the city and his councillor Pieter Lanchals was beheaded. Lanchals' coat of arms featured a swan (the family name is derived from '*lang hals*': long neck), and the emperor ordered that swans be kept on the canals of Bruges for evermore, as a reminder of the city's dreadful crime.

respite from the tour-boat microphones. The canal traces an arc from here to the 't Zand in the west of the city: wander or cycle along its route (although the road does depart from the bank at times) in the early morning or at dusk to glimpse a golden-hued and lesser-visited Bruges. It follows Spaanse Loskaai, the quay where Spanish ships used to unload their cargo, including Castil-lian wool to replace the increasingly rare English product, for Flemish weavers to transform into the finest cloth in Europe.

Augustijnenbrug
Bus: 3, 13; map p.132 C1
Crossing from Spaanse Loskaai to Augustijnenrei is the triple-arched Augustijnen-brug (Augustinians' Bridge), the first stone bridge in Bruges, built 1294 by monks from the former – you

guessed it – Augustinian friary on the north side of the canal. A modern apartment block now occupies the site of the friary. Legend has it there was once a secret tunnel under the canal through which the monks would reach a convent on the opposite bank, for illicit trysts with nuns. The house on the corner of Span-jaardstraat by the bridge – Den Noodt Gods, built 1616 by Spanish merchant Fran-cisco de Peralta – has been known since the 19th century as the Spookhuis, inspired by

Below: the three arches of the Augustijnenbrug.

stories of a monk who killed the object of his devotion in a fit of passion. Their two spirits allegedly haunt the building, which has changed hands repeatedly, and been abandoned on more than one occasion.

Vlamingbrug

Bus: 3, 13; map p.132 B1

Built in 1331 as a continuation of the busy thoroughfare leading to the artists' district to the north, this two-arched bridge leads to the pretty Pottenmakersstraat.

Groenerei

Bus: 6, 16; map p.135 D4

The stretch of canal along Groenerei is one of the most picturesque. Admire the back gardens of the lucky residents who live alongside it.

Meebrug and Peerdenbrug

Bus: 0/Centrum, 6, 16; map p.135 C4–D4

The grey stone of these two bridges along Groenerei is softened by a covering of foliage. Their single arches reflected in the canal frame a shimmering image of quay-

Near Ezelbrug (Donkey Bridge), along Grauwwerkersstraat, there remains a fine stretch of old city wall, including part of a defensive tower dating from 1127 in the back garden of one of the houses (best viewed from across the water in Pottenmakersstraat). These original city walls were thrown up around the inner canal circuit in the aftermath of Charles the Good's assassination. Their purpose was to defend what was then a much smaller city than that enclosed by the second line of circumvallation, whose outline dates from the 14th century and is preserved today by the ring canal and a park.

side houses. Do not miss the view from Peerdenbrug along to the tower of Sint-Salvatorskathedraal.

Jan van Eyckplein

Bus: 4, 14; map p.133 C1

Bruges has many former harbours, and this one – along adjoining Spiegelrei – was the busiest of them all;

the canal that terminates here once led as far as the Markt. Along here came boats laden with Castillian oranges and lemons, Oriental spices, Mediterranean velvet and brocade, Baltic fur and amber. This was also the commercial and diplomatic centre for medieval Bruges, with foreign consulates situated along the length of Spiegelrei.

Langerei

Bus: 4, 14; map p.133 D4–C1

In the Middle Ages, this would have been one of the city's busiest canal thoroughfares, between the Dampoort and the canal to Damme and the merchants' quarter along Spiegelrei. Right up until World War II, coal, wheat and wood were unloaded down here. Today, however, a relaxing canalside stroll up either side – along the street named Langerei or Potterierei opposite – offers a glimpse of 'ordinary' Bruges, and it is indicative of this city's great beauty that it lacks little, or nothing, of the

Below: the much-photographed Rozenhoedkaai.

Above: the attractive Duinenbrug is a wooden drawbridge.

splendour of better-advertised locations. The Potterierei (east) side is a slightly quieter road, and is sunny in the afternoon.

Carmersbrug
Bus: 4, 14; map p.133 C1
Look down from this bridge to the wall by the water where a modern stone statue of a Carmelite monk holds a staff to measure the water's depth.

Duinenbrug
Bus: 4, 14; map p.133 D3
This small wooden drawbridge, towards the top of the Potterierei near the Groot-Seminarie, is supported on two stone arches, and makes this part of the canal seem distinctly less urban.

Early tourists to Bruges would have arrived by luxury barge from Ghent, Nieuwpoort or Ostend and alighted at the Bargehuis (barge house), now a bar, near the Katelijnebrug swing bridge. Many of today's tourists also arrive in this neck of the woods, just down the Bargeweg in the main coach park.

Minnewater
Bus: 1; map p.134 C1
The Minnewater is not just a pretty lake with weeping willows; it also serves a practical purpose: water for the canals enters the city here, fed from the Ghent and perimeter canals. The pink brick lockhouse (Sashuis; 1519), which overlooks the long rectangular basin, regulates the level of the canals in the city centre.

The name Minnewater (often translated as 'Lake of Love') seems to be a mistranslation of an earlier name for this stretch of water, which once served as an interior port; the Binnenwater. As many as 150 seagoing ships and canal barges loaded and unloaded cargo here daily before the river silted up and they had to stop at Damme. Boats would dock here before sailing on into Flanders and to Ghent.
SEE ALSO PARKS AND GARDENS, P.105

Rozenhoedkaai
Bus: 1, 11, 6, 16; map p.135 C4
The view over the canal from Rozenhoedkaai (Rosary Quay) graces many a postcard. It follows the line of the River Dijver, the old waterside houses and the Belfort (Belfry). Winston Churchill is one of the many artists, amateur and professional, who have painted the scene from this spot. It is also where the maudlin protagonist of Georges Rodenbach's novel *Bruges-la-Morte* lived: 'He would spend the whole day in his room, a vast retreat on the first floor whose windows looked out onto the Quai du Rosaire, along which the facade of his house stretched, mirrored in the canal.' The location also inspired the 1906 poem *Quai du Rosaire* by Rainer Maria Rilke, a Rodenbach admirer.
SEE ALSO LITERATURE AND THEATRE, P.74

Bonifaciusbrugje
Bus: 0/Centrum; map p.134 C3
This scenic footbridge across the canal behind the Arentshuis and Gruuthuse Museum is a majestic example of the Gothic revival in Bruges. It was built in 1910 but could have been here for centuries from the patina of its stone. It bridges a cool green stretch of canal flanked by vine-covered houses and a rare surviving timber facade.

Sint-Jan Nepomucenusbrug
Bus: 0/Centrum, 1, 11, 6, 16; map p.135 C3
This bridge (also known as Eekhoutbrug) across the Dijver, a canalised offshoot of the Reie river, is crowned by the imposing statue of St John of Nepomuk (1767), which stands between two wrought-iron lamps. St John, patron saint and protector against flooding, was thrown in the Moldau in Prague in 1393 by King Wenceslas IV.

41

Children

Bruges may be best known for its churches and museums, but there is still plenty to keep children entertained, both in the city or at the many attractions in the surrounding countryside and nearby coast. The compact size of the place and relative absence of traffic make it a much less tiring destination for kids than many city trips, and the canals and bridges add to its appeal. As well as the selection of child-friendly museums, monuments, parks and theme-parks described in alphabetical order below, young ones are also sure to enjoy the pancakes, waffles, hot chocolate and chips that are local specialities.

Accommodation

Most hotels have family rooms or will provide a child's bed on request. It is always worth phoning beforehand to check this sort of detailed information.

Coast

The coast near Bruges has wide and safe sandy beaches, dunes, and a gentle gradient into the sea. Most resorts have child-friendly markers along the beach – bright-coloured animals on posts – so that children can easily locate the spot where their family is sitting. **De Haan** has a mini-golf course and a small enclosure with goats and rabbits, and here and in other resorts there are many places that rent out pedal-powered buggies for driving along the promenade, as well as bikes. At **Ostend** there is a good museum aboard a former Icelandic trawler and a navy training ship, the *Mercator*, open to visitors in the attractive town-centre marina. A ride on the **kusttram** (coast tram) is also fun, although parents – and, indeed, anyone – should be

extra careful when crossing the coast road at any point, as the tram travels very fast down the central reservation, and accidents are not uncommon.
SEE ALSO THE COAST, P.20–1

Eating Out

Taking children to restaurants is standard practice in Belgium in all except the most upmarket places. Most brasseries, cafés and lower-priced establishments have children's menus, or will adapt their dishes to suit. Children will like the *croque-monsieur* (toasted ham and cheese sandwich; with an egg on top: *croque-madame*), omelettes, plates of ham and cheese chunks that most bars serve as snacks, and the tiny North Sea shrimps, which are served stuffed in tomatoes or deep-fried in a white sauce *(garnalkroketten)*.

Festivals and Events

Meifoor

't Zand; late Apr–late May; bus: 0/Centrum; map p.134 A3
A sprawling funfair sets up on the 't Zand square and Koning Albertpark every May,

with dozens of stalls and rides for all ages.

Snow and Ice Brugge

Stationsplein; www.ijs sculptuur.be; late Nov–early Jan, check website for dates; daily 10am–7pm; bus: 0/Centrum; map p.134 B1
Each winter over the Christmas period, a large ice sculpture festival takes place in tents in front of the station, with buildings, figures and animals crafted by dozens of professional ice artists who travel from northern climes. The theme changes each year and is always very child-friendly, although kids will need to be wrapped up warm. There is a heated drinks tent in which to thaw out at the end. An ice-skating rink takes up residence on the Markt square throughout the festive season from the last week of November until the first week of January; children will also like the Christmas market with fairground carousels on the Markt and Simon Stevinplein.

Indoor Play Centres

Speeldorp

Diksmuidestraat 5, Blanken-

Left: friendly faces at the Boudewijn Sea Park.

building just west of the city centre, with a large café area.

Monuments
Belfort
Markt 7; tel: 050 44 81 11; www.brugge.be/musea; daily 9.30am–5pm; entrance charge; bus: 0/Centrum; map p.134 C4
Not for tiny children, but for those who can manage 366 steps up a narrow, steep and often crowded spiral stair-case. The experience is well worth it, and the view from the top spectacular.
SEE ALSO MONUMENTS, P.78

Sint-Janshuismolen and Other Windmills
Kruisvest; tel: 050 44 81 11; www.brugge.be/musea; Apr–Sept Tue–Sat 9.30am–12.30pm, 1.30–5pm; entrance charge; bus: 6, 16; map p.133 E2
The knowledgeable atten-dants demonstrate how an old grain mill works, and as long as there is a little wind you can watch it make flour. There is a rather steep climb up the steps to the windmill.
SEE ALSO MONUMENTS, P.80

Museums and Galleries
The following are particularly suited to children:
Choco-Story
Wijnzakstraat 2; tel: 050 61 22 37; www.choco-story.be; daily 10am–5pm; entrance charge; bus: 0/Centrum, 6, 16; map p.132 C1
Children aged 6–12 can play the Choclala sticker game provided at the entrance to this museum about the history and traditions of chocolate-making. There is a gift on the way out for all those who complete the game correctly.
SEE ALSO MUSEUMS AND GALLERIES, P.89

Groeningemuseum
Dijver 12; tel: 050 44 87 11;

Entrance to all city-owned museums (the 'Bruggemuseum', which include the Belfort, Groeninge, Volkskunde, etc.) is free to children under 13. For most other attractions, entry is free for children under 3.

---

berge; tel: 050 34 84 27; www.speeldorp.be; Wed, Sat–Sun 1–6pm, daily during school holidays; entrance charge; bus: 14; map p.132 B4
An indoor play centre with bouncy castles, climbing frames and slides for small children; plus lots of tables and chairs for adults.

De Toverplaneet
Legeweg 88; tel: 0478 22 69 29; www.detoverplaneet.be; Wed 1–8pm, Fri 3.30–8pm, Sat–Sun 10.30am–8pm, school holidays daily 10.30am–8pm, closed on hot summer days; entrance charge (adults free); bus: 9
Space-themed play centre with a climbing structure and chutes in a former industrial

Below: parent-powered buggies on the coastal promenade.

Above: mother and babies in Minnewater park.

www.brugge.be/musea; Tue–Sun 9.30am–5pm; entrance charge; bus: 0/Centrum; map p.134 C3
The modern art in the collection may interest children, but there is also a children's corner and play house designed to keep them entertained while their parents look at the works of van Eyck, Bosch and other Flemish Primitives.
SEE ALSO MUSEUMS AND GALLERIES, P.85

Bruggemuseum-Volkskunde
Balstraat 43; tel: 050 44 87 11; www.brugge.be/musea; Tue–Sun 9.30am–5pm; entrance charge; bus: 6, 16; map p.133 D1
The folklore museum makes for a fascinating visit, particularly for children, and a way to get an idea of how people in Bruges lived around 200 years ago. A row of tiny almshouses contains re-creations of the interiors of old shops – including a chemist, clogmaker and hatter, plus many more – as well as a schoolroom and several family homes. In fair weather, there are traditional toys to play with in the garden and sweet-making demonstrations are held in the candy

shop on Thursday afternoons.
SEE ALSO MUSEUMS AND GALLERIES, P.90

Parks and Gardens
Beisbroek
Zeeweg, Sint-Andries; www.beisbroek.be; nature centre: Apr–Nov Mon–Fri 2–5pm, Sun 2–6pm, Mar Sun 2–6pm; planetarium shows: Wed and Sun 3pm and 4.30pm, Fri 8.30pm; school holidays also Mon, Tue, Thur 3pm; free (charge for observatory); bus: 52, 53; map p.138 C3
Outdoor attractions at this large country park include a deer compound; indoors there is a nature centre, observatory and planetarium.
SEE ALSO PARKS AND GARDENS, P.107

Hof Sebrechts
entrances on Beenhouwersstraat and Oude Zak; bus: 9, 41,

For swimming, both the **Provinciaal Zwembad Olympiabad** (Doornstraat 110, Sint-Andries; tel: 050 39 02 00; map p.138 C3) and **Intercommunaal Zwembad Interbad** (Veltemweg 35; tel: 050 35 07 77) have slides.

42; map p.134 B4
Attractions for kids in this tranquil park include a sandpit, playground and regular sculpture exhibitions. The park is behind the houses so it is not bordered by roads.
SEE ALSO PARKS AND GARDENS, P.104

Koningin Astridpark
Minderbroederstraat; bus: 1, 11; map p.135 D3
As well as a children's play area and a pond, this park has lots of trees and space to run around; it is not too large and the church in the corner of the park makes it easy to get your bearings. The Estaminet café alongside is popular with families, too.
SEE ALSO PARKS AND GARDENS, P.105

Minnewater
Minnewater; bus: 1; map p.134 C1
Kids will like the lake with all its ducks, geese and swans, and the magical-looking Minnewater castle along the banks of the lake. At the end of the park, on Wijngaardplein, is the horse fountain, a popular spot, where the horses that pull the carriages around town wait in line to take a drink and munch some hay.
SEE ALSO PARKS AND GARDENS, P.105

Provinciaal Domein Tillegembos
Tillegemstraat 83, 8200 Sint-Andries; tel: 050 40 35 43; bus: 25; map p.138 C3
An extensive park with woodland, playgrounds and a moated castle, just to the south of Bruges.

De Zeven Torentjes
Canadaring 41, 8310 Assebroek; tel: 050 35 40 43; daily 8am–dusk; free; bus: 2 Sint-Lucas/Assebroek; map p.139 C3
This country estate on the outskirts of Bruges has been turned into a dedicated children's farm with pigs, hens, horses, rabbits and more.

Sun Parks, a holiday village near De Haan, has a number of special child-friendly chalets among its choice of accommodation, and the whole complex is car-free. There is an indoor children's play area for under-13s, and a large leisure pool area – Aquafun – which is also open to non-residents. *See* www.sunparks.be; coast tram (stop Sun Parks).

There are also demonstrations by a blacksmith, some educational programmes and horse-and-cart rides.

Theme Parks

Boudewijn Sea Park
A. De Baeckestraat 12, 8200 Bruges; tel: 050 38 38 38; www.boudewijnseapark.be; Apr and Sept Sat–Sun 10am–5pm, Easter school holiday, May–June Thur–Tue 10am–5pm, July–Aug daily 10am–6pm; entrance charge, free for children under 1m (3ft) tall, reduced price for children under 13; bus: 7, 17
Sea park with dolphinarium in the southern suburbs of Bruges (2.5km/1½ miles from rail station) that is a big favourite with children and adults. Plenty of rides and boats, as well as regular shows with dolphins and orca (killer whale).

Seafront Zeebrugge
Vismijnstraat 7; tel: 050 55 14 15; www.seafront.be; July–Aug daily 10am–7pm, Sept–June daily 10am–6pm, closed 2 weeks in Jan; entrance charge (children under 1m, free); train: Zeebrugge Kerk (then 100m/yd walk); map p.138 C4
A maritime theme park-cum-museum ideal for a half-day visit. There are interactive exhibits, videos, a pirates play-ship, a real lightship and the prize exhibit, a 100m (330ft) -long Soviet Foxtrot submarine, built 1960, in

which visitors can experience a 4-min sound-and-light show simulating an attack. Free parking.

Tours

BIKE TOURS
Quasimundo Bike Tours
Nieuwe Gentweg 5; tel: 050 33 07 75; www.quasimundo.com; tours run Mar–Oct daily 9.50am, starting at Toyo Ito pavilion on the Burg (reservation required); entrance charge; map p.134 C2
Quasimundo has a huge stock of bikes in all sizes, as well as safety helmets and child seats. Children under the age of eight go free. The guides are knowledgeable and entertaining.

BOAT TOURS
Katelijnestraat 4; tel: 050 33 27 71; www.nvstael.com; Mar–Nov 10am–6pm; entrance charge; bus: 0/Centrum; map p.134 C2
Boat tours around the canals of Bruges are fun for children, as the small boats hug the water and skim under very low bridges. There are several starting points in the city – behind the Onze-Lieve-Vrouwekerk (the company listed above departs from here), along the Dijver,

Below: cycling in Bruges is fun and safe for everyone.

beside the Vismarkt and on the Rozenhoedkaai.
HORSE-DRAWN CARRIAGES
Markt; tel: 050 34 54 01; www.hippo.be/koets; daily 9.30am–5.30pm; entrance charge; bus: 0/Centrum (Markt); map p.134 C4
There is room for up to five adults in one of the horse-drawn carriages that tour the streets of Bruges. Each tour lasts around 35 mins, including a drink-stop for the horse at the Begijnhof, where passengers can get off and visit. The carriages depart from the Markt daily except Wednesday – market day, when they decamp to the Burg.
PADDLE STEAMER TRIPS
Bruges-Damme
Damme tourist office; tel: 050 28 86 10; www.toerismedamme.be; 1 Apr–15 Oct five departures each way per day; entrance charge; bus: 4; map p.139 C3
The *Lamme Goedzak* stern-wheel paddle-steamer moors in Bruges at Noorweegse Kaai 31, just beyond Dampoort, and departs several times a day for Damme, 7km (4 miles) away, before making the return trip, half an hour each way.

Below: horse-powered carriages tour the town.

Churches

Ever since Flemish knight Dirk of Alsace returned to Bruges from the Second Crusade in 1150 with what was said to be a relic of the blood of Christ, the city has been a centre of pilgrimage and great piety: various religious communities flourished and churches grew rich with the gifts of foreign merchants and other wealthy benefactors. As a result, there are treasures aplenty behind the doors of most places of worship in the city; and seeking out these historic artworks and artefacts is to take a fascinating journey back in time to the golden age of medieval Bruges.

Markt and Burg

Heilig Bloedbasiliek (Basilica of the Holy Blood)
Burg; tel: 050 33 67 92; www.holyblood.com; Apr–Sept 9.30am–noon, 2–6pm, Oct–Mar Thur–Tue 10am–noon, 2–4pm, Wed 10am–noon; free; bus: 0/Centrum; map p.134 C4

Named after the relic of Christ's blood that it was built to house, the Heilig Bloedbasiliek has been a place of pilgrimage for centuries. Its three-arched facade, completed in 1534, has ornate stone carvings and gilded statues of angels, knights and their ladies, below two towers of great delicacy. The interior is divided into two chapels, a 12th-century Romanesque lower chapel and a more recent Gothic upper chapel, providing a dramatic contrast in styles.

THE LOWER CHAPEL
The lower chapel is a study in shadows, with austere, unadorned lines, Romanesque pillars, and little decoration except for a relief carving over an interior door-way depicting the baptism of St Basil (an early Church Father). St Basil's relics were brought back from Palestine by Robert II, the Count of Flanders. The faded carving, which dates from around 1150, is naïve in style, and this is emphasised by the two mismatched columns supporting it. In the right nave, the wooden statue of a Virgin and Child has been venerated since the 14th century. The wooden trap door in the floor led to the tomb of 14th-century master stonemason Jan van Oudenaerde.

THE UPPER CHAPEL
Access to the upper chapel is through a beautiful Late Gothic doorway. Ascending by the broad, well-worn 16th-century spiral staircase, you can enter the upper chapel beneath the organ case. The lines of the chapel may have been spoiled somewhat by over-eager 19th-century decoration and murals, but the impression is of warmth and richness. The ceiling looks like an upturned boat and the room is flooded with a golden light. The bronze-coloured pul-

On Ascension Day every year, the relic of the holy blood is carried through Bruges in the famous Heilig-Bloed Processie (Procession of the Holy Blood), the most important of West Flanders' festivals. The venerated phial is transported in a flamboyant gold and silver reliquary that is normally kept in the treasury of the chapel.

pit is a curious sight, bearing a remarkable resemblance to a cored and stuffed tomato.

In a small side chapel you will find the holy relic from which the church derives its name. Flemish knight Dirk of Alsace returned from the Second Crusade in the Holy Land in 1149 and is said to have brought with him a crystal phial believed to contain some drops of Christ's blood. Soon venerated all over medieval Europe, it is still brought out each Friday afternoon for the faithful. The dried blood turned to liquid at regular intervals for many years, an event declared to be a miracle by Pope Clement V. The phial is stored in a richly ornate silver taber-

Left: upper chapel of the Basilica of the Holy Blood.

exterior is a hotchpotch of different styles, but the interior is filled with treasures. Chief among them is the marble *Madonna and Child* (1504) by Michelangelo, originally intended for Siena Cathedral and the only one of the sculptor's works to have travelled outside Italy during his lifetime. It was brought to Bruges by a Flemish merchant, Jan van Moeskroen. The Madonna is a subdued, preoccupied figure, while the infant leans nonchalantly on her knee.

There are some fine paintings here by Pieter Pourbus (*Last Supper* and *Adoration of the Shepherds*) and Gerard David (*Transfiiguration*), but it is the chancel area that holds most interest, after the Michelangelo. Here you can see the tombs of Charles the Bold and his daughter Mary of Burgundy, fine examples of, respectively, Renaissance and Late Gothic carving. Both sarcophagi are richly decorated with coats of arms linked with floral motifs in

nacle presented by the archdukes of Spain in 1611. It is carried in a grand procession through the streets every year on Ascension Day.
SEE ALSO ARCHITECTURE, P.24; MUSEUMS AND GALLERIES, P.82

South
Begijnhofkerk
Begijnhof; tel: 050 33 00 11; daily 7am–12.15pm, 3–6pm; free; bus: 1; map p.134 B2
The Begijnhofkerk (the church of the Begijnhof) is lesser known under its official name, Onze-Lieve-Vrouw van Troost van Spermalie (Our Lady of Consolation of Spermalie) and dates from 1245, although it was rebuilt in 1605 after a fire, then given a baroque makeover around 1700. The only object saved from the fire is a wooden (now gilded) statue of the Madonna (1300) on the side altar; an original Romanesque door is also visible on the north facade. Services held by the convent nuns are open to the public and include Gregorian sung offices.
SEE ALSO BEGUINAGES, P.29; MUSEUMS AND GALLERIES, P.84

Onze-Lieve-Vrouwekerk
Mariastraat; Mon–Fri 9.30am–12.30pm, 1.30–5pm, Sat 9.30am–12.30pm, 1.30–4pm, Sun 1.30–5pm; free (entrance charge to parts of the church); bus: 1; map p.134 C3
The vertiginous brick spire of Onze-Lieve-Vrouwekerk (Church of our Lady) makes this the city's tallest landmark, recognisable across the flat polders around Bruges. The

Below: towering spire of Onze-Lieve-Vrouwekerk.

47

C

Above: exquisite *Madonna and Child* by Michelangelo.

copper-gilt, gold, reds and blues; the figures themselves (with domestic details like the pet dogs at Mary's feet) are also in copper gilt. However, whether or not Charles and Mary are actually buried here is a matter of some dispute. Charles died in battle in Nancy in 1477 and it was difficult to identify the body. Mary, who died in a riding accident at the age of 25 (bringing to a close the 100-year reign of the House of Burgundy), may in fact be buried among a group of polychrome tombs in the

Michelangelo's *Madonna and Child* in the Onze-Lieve-Vrouwekerk is a rare work by the artist would have left Italy. It did so by accident, sold to a Flemish merchant after the Italian family who commissioned it for Siena Cathedral failed to pay the artist. Walpole tried, unsuccessfully, to buy it for England in the 18th century; the French whisked it away to Paris during the Revolution; and the Germans swiped it in World War II.

choir that were discovered in 1979. You can see the frescoed tombs beneath your feet through windows in the floor and by means of mirrors in front of the sarcophagi.

Elsewhere in the church, you will find the funerary chapel of Pieter Lanchals – fated advisor to Maximilian of Austria, killed by the angry citizens of Bruges – containing frescoed tombs in maroon and black, as well as Van Dyck's starkly atmospheric painting of Christ on the Cross. The splendid wooden gallery overlooking the chancel belongs to the adjacent Gruuthuse mansion and dates from the 15th century.
SEE ALSO ARCHITECTURE, P.24; MUSEUMS AND GALLERIES, P.86

West
Karmelietenkerk
Ezelstraat 28; tel: 050 44 38 89; www.priorij.be; Mon–Fri 8am–11.30am, 3–5.30pm; free; bus: 3; map p.132 B1
The 15th-century Karmelietenkerk (Carmelite Church) belonged to the big Carmelite Monastery that has occupied the former Hof van Uitkerke here since 1633. The baroque interior dates from 1688–91 and is a peaceful place. The monastery is an unusual-looking building, perhaps because it was built by monks who were involved with the care of plague victims at the time. The Carmelites were expelled by the French in 1795 but returned in the 19th century, and the church is one of the few places in Bruges which is occupied by religious men and women and where you are likely to catch sight of any of them. Every Sunday at 10am there is a sung Gregorian Mass; the church is also regularly used for concerts.

Foundations of the old cathedral of St Donatian's can be viewed in the basement of the Crowne Plaza hotel on the Burg. These were discovered and preserved during works on the hotel in the 1990s; access is free to visitors. The Toyo Ito Pavilion on the square occupies the site of the former church, which was destroyed after the French Revolution; it stands in a circle of gravel that demarcates the cathedral's central chapel.

Onze-Lieve-Vrouw-van-Blindekens
Kreupelenstraat, daily 2–5pm; free; bus: 0/Centrum ('t Zand); map p.134 A3
Just outside the main city perimeter but worth a look if you are in the neighbourhood on a tour of all the city's almshouses, Onze-Lieve-Vrouw-van-Blindekens (Our Lady of the Blind) is a bright and simple 17th-century church. Its founding honours a promise made at the battle of Mons-en-Pévèle in 1304, against the French. It has a carved pulpit from 1659 and, most notably, a gilded 14th-century statue of the Madonna and Child above a side altar. The chapel is the departure point for the annual Feast of the Assumption procession held on 15 August, wending its way to the church of Onze-Lieve-Vrouw-ter-Potterie (Our Lady of the Pottery).
Sint-Jakobskerk
Sint-Jakobsstraat; Apr–30 Sept Mon–Sat 10am–noon, 2–5pm, Sun 2–5pm; free; bus: 0/Centrum; map p.132 B1
Built 1220 over an earlier chapel, Sint-Jakobskerk (St James's Church) was quickly enlarged into a three-naved Gothic hall-church. It grew incredibly wealthy during the 15th century, thanks to generous endowments from parish-

Above: colourful stained glass in Sint-Salvatorskathedraal.

ioners, including wealthy merchants and the residents of the Duke of Burgundy's Prinsenhof. The 18 altars around the church were each sponsored by a trade guild or corporation: note Lancelot Blondeel's 1523 altarpiece, made for the surgeons' and barbers' corporation.

A number of Flemish Primitive masterpieces were painted for this church, including works by Hans Memling, Hugo van der Goes and Roger van der Weyden. These have been removed, with one exception: the triptych of *The Legend of St Lucy* (1480). Painted by an anonymous contemporary of Memling known as the Master of the Legend of St Lucy, it is located in St Anthony's Chapel, and tells the story of a wealthy Sicilian virgin who, in gratitude for the recovery of her sick mother after her pilgrimage to St Agatha's tomb, gave all her worldly goods to the poor. This did not please the man to whom she was betrothed and he had her condemned to

death. There are also two triptychs by Pieter Pourbus, and the mausoleum of Ferry de Gros (1544), treasurer of the Order of the Golden Fleece, which is one of the finest examples of Flemish Renaissance sculpture.

Sint-Salvatorskathedraal
Zuidzandstraat; tel: 050 33 68 41; www.sintsalvator.be; Mon 2–5.45pm, Tue–Fri 8.30–11.45am, 2–5.45pm, Sat 8.30–11.45am, 2–3.30pm, Sun 9–10.15am, 2–5pm; closed to casual visitors during services; museum: Sun–Fri 2–5pm, free except museum; bus: 0/Centrum; map p.134 B3

Bruges' original parish church, dating from the 9th century, Sint-Salvatorskathedraal (Holy Saviour's Cathedral) only became the cathedral in 1834, replacing the Burg square's St Donatian's, which had been destroyed by the French in the late 18th century. The structure is mainly Gothic in style (13th–16th century), having succumbed to several fires, but it retains some

Romanesque elements. Its brick belfry rises 100m, and, with the spire of Onze Lieve Vrouwekerk and the Halletoren, is a principal feature on the Bruges skyline.

The 15th-century wooden choir stalls flanking the altar bear a complete set of escutcheons of the Knights of the Golden Fleece, who held a chapter meeting here in 1478. Other notable features are the baroque rood-screen surmounted by the sculpture *God the Father*, by Antwerp artist Artus Quellin, the elaborate pulpit and the 18th-century tapestries beside the altar.
SEE ALSO MUSEUMS AND GALLERIES, P.88

North

Sint-Gilliskerk
Sint-Gilliskerkhof; Apr–Sept Mon–Sat 10am–noon, 2–5pm, Sun 2–5pm; free; bus: 4, 14; map p.133 C2

The parish church of Sint-Gilliskerk (St Giles' Church), a neo-Gothic church founded in 1241 and built in the early Gothic style, was drastically altered in the 15th century, leaving it with three aisles in place of the earlier cruciform shape. Now an edifice of agreeably stout proportions and with a brick tower similar to that of Sint-Salvatorskathedraal, only the chunky stone pillars inside date from the original construction. Among the treasures to be seen within are a superb organ, a polyptych (1564) by Pieter Pourbus, and a cycle of paintings from 1774 by Bruges artist Jan Garemijn depicting the history of the Trinitarian Brothers, and their retrieval of white slaves from Algeria. The painter Hans Memling was buried here in 1494 in the no longer extant churchyard, and is remembered on a plaque beside the entrance. **49**

Above: Sint-Jakobskerk's interior is filled with treasures *(see p.48)*.

Sint-Walburgakerk

Sint Maartensplein; Apr–Oct
Mon–Sat 10am–noon, 2–5pm,
Sun 2–5pm; free; bus: 0/
Centrum, 6, 16; map p.133 C1

This oratory was built in
1619–42 by the Jesuits, who
had moved into Bruges in
force after the Spanish
authorities crushed the
Calvinists in 1584. They set
up base around here, building
a monastery, a college and
this church, which is all that
survived their suppression in
1774. There is not much
space in front of the building
to stand back and admire its
orderly dimensions, but there
are treasures aplenty in the
cool interior, flooded with
silvery light by two decks of
pale grey stained-glass windows reflected in the black-
and-white marble floor tiles.
Probably the most remark-
able is the carved Carrara
marble communion rail that
stretches across the width of
the three marble altars. There
is also a fabulously over-the-
top oak pulpit (1669) by Artus
Quellin the Younger, which
has twin stairways with a
scalloped canopy uplifted by
trumpeting angels. Anything
but discreet, this nevertheless

survived the French Revolution, when the church was
transformed into a temple of
law. The triptych on the right-
hand wall, *Our Lady of the
Dry Tree* (1620), portrays the
apparition of the Virgin to
Philip the Good as he prayed
before his victory against the
French. It is the work of Pieter
Claeissens the Younger.

Today the church is the
venue for concerts of classical and church music during
the Festival of Flanders.
SEE ALSO ARCHITECTURE, P.26

East

Engels Klooster

Carmersstraat 85; tel: 050 33 24
24; www.the-english-
convent.be; Mon–Sat 2–3.45pm,
4.15–5.30pm; free; bus: 4, 14;
map p.133 D2

The Engels Klooster (English
convent) houses a commu-
nity of Augustinian sisters
and was established in the
wake of England's Dissolu-
tion of the Monasteries under
King Henry VIII. Its imposing
dome dates from the first half
of the 18th century. Anne
Mary Edmonstone was sent
here to complete her educa-
tion and to convert to
Catholicism in order to marry

pioneering naturalist Charles
Waterton (1782–1865),
founder of the world's first
nature reserve. The convent
has an historically important
library of English books and
runs a guesthouse.

Jeruzalemkerk

Peperstraat; tel: 050 33 00 72;
www.kantcentrum.com; Mon–
Fri 10am–noon, 2–6pm, Sat till
5pm; entrance charge (includes
entry to Lace Centre); bus: 6, 16;
map p.133 D1

The striking Jeruzalemkerk
was built between 1428 and
1465 and is a curious combination of Byzantine and
Gothic styles. It was built by
the Adornes family, originally
merchants from Genoa, who
had travelled on a pilgrimage
to Jerusalem and were so
impressed by the Church of
the Holy Sepulchre that they
built a copy of it in Bruges.
There is even a copy of
Christ's memorial tomb in the
crypt. Spared pillage or
destruction throughout the
centuries thanks to its private
chapel status – the church is
is still owned by the family's
descendants – it is remark-
ably well preserved.

The lofty interior is sombre
and laden with symbols of

mourning and penitence, and with very good examples of 15th- and 16th-century stained glass, some of which depicts members of the Adornes family. The space is dominated by the mausoleum of Anselm Adornes, and his wife, Marguerite van der Banck. Other family members are buried beneath the church, and their shields adorn the mausoleum. Anselm (b.1424) was burgomaster of Bruges, but was murdered in Scotland in 1483 while on a consular mission. Although buried in Linlithgow, his heart was brought back to Bruges in a lead box to be laid to rest beside his wife.

The altar is carved in a rather macabre fashion, with skulls and bones, and the cave-like atmosphere of the church is emphasised by the space behind the altar and above the crypt, which rises almost to the full height of the tower to create a rather eerie cavern.

Atop the tower outside sit the Jerusalem cross, and the wheel and palm leaf of St Catherine, to commemorate the journey of Anselm and his son to Jerusalem and Mt Sinai in 1470.

Onze-Lieve-Vrouw-ter-Potterie

Potterierei 79; Tue–Sun 9.30am–12.30pm, 1.30–5pm; free except adjoining museum; bus: 4; map p.133 D3

The 14th-century Onze-Lieve-Vrouw-ter-Potterie (Our Lady of the Pottery) used to be the chapel of the Potters' Guild, and is a little gem. It started life as part of a hospice, founded in 1276 by Augustinian nuns and became a retirement home in the 15th century (a large part of the complex retains this role today). A former ward of the hospice and the cloisters are

Ignatius de Loyola, the Spanish priest who founded the Jesuit Order in Paris in 1534 (it was formally approved by the Pope in 1540), was a frequent guest of Spanish merchant Gonzalez d'Aguilera between 1528 and 1530, in his house at No. 9 Spanjaardstraat. Loyola was also in regular contact in Bruges with the Spanish-born humanist philosopher Juan Luis Vivés (1492–1540), a statue of whom stands behind the Onze-Lieve-Vrouwekerk beside the Bonifaciusbrugje.

now the Potterie-museum.

The oldest part of the church is the left-hand nave, dating from 1359. Its two side altars are adorned with embroidered hangings made of gold and silver thread (c.1565). The choir altarpiece is an *Adoration of the Shepherds* by 17th-century local artist Jacob van Oost the Elder. In the right nave stands what is said to be the oldest Netherlandish miracle statue, Our Lady of Mons-en-Pévèle, crafted in wood in the early 14th century and named after

the 1305 battle of the same name. The 16th-century tapestries flanking the left side of the right nave depict miracles associated with the Virgin Mary reproduced in a lively style reminiscent of 16th-century daily life.
SEE ALSO MUSEUMS AND GALLERIES, P.91

Sint-Annakerk

Sint-Annaplein; Apr–Sept Mon–Sat 10am–noon, 2–5pm, Sun 2–5pm; free; bus: 6, 16; map p.133 D1

Enclosed by an elegant square, Sint-Annakerk (Church of St Anne) is a 1624 baroque replacement for the Gothic church destroyed by fire in 1561. Inside, the carving of the rood screen, confessionals and pulpit, as well as the rich panelling, are all well worth viewing. The mural depicting the *Last Judgement* (1685) is by Henri Herregoudts. The counter on the left as you enter used to be where the poor of the parish would sign (or make a mark) each time they attended Mass, so they could receive tokens to exchange for food and clothing on feast days.

Below: high brick walls hung with escutcheons in Jeruzalemkerk.

Environment

Bruges has little to complain about when it comes to the environment. Refreshed by North Sea winds; encircled by grassy fields reclaimed from the sea centuries ago for farming, and the icon of affluent Flanders, it has become a model of sustainable town planning, served by excellent public transport and flat enough to encourage anyone to hop on a bike. The only serious threats to the environment are found on the outskirts of the city and around Zeebrugge port, where pressure to pave over swathes of countryside has provoked fierce local protest and the creation of a militant 'green belt' movement.

Clean Water

Everyone loves the canals in Bruges. What few people know is that, until 1980, much of the city's waste water was dumped directly into them. A lot has changed since then: the waters are so clean now that even the fish have returned.

No private boats besides the tourist boats are allowed on the inner canals, and locks at the city borders are kept closed to prevent dirtier water from the Ghent and Ostend canals entering the inner canal system. To help the water stay clean, a water aeration system is used at the Coupure lock and the Ezelpoort fountain.

Properties that border the canals do not suffer the same level of degradation as canal-side houses in areas of tidal, sea water (such as Venice), but to allow residents to maintain their properties below the waterline, the city regularly lowers the water level by up to 1m (3ft), on request. This is done during the winter months when the tourist boats stop operating.

Above: cycling is the greenest way to get around the city.

Energy

The brisk winds off the North Sea make the flat polders around Bruges ideal for harnessing wind energy; the turbines visible from the Belfort are along the canal to Zeebrugge. Other renewable energy projects in the region include a thriving business by local food and farming producers to transform their waste into biogas, which they then sell to the national electricity grid. Homeowners,

meanwhile, can get subsidies to install double glazing, solar thermal panels and energy-efficient boilers.

Green Belt

Recent years have seen the growth of a 'green belt' movement in an effort to stem development on greenfield sites around the edge of the city. The movement grew out of fierce opposition, five years ago, to a plan to build offices and a road through the Lappersfortbos, on the edge of Bruges. This woodland area was occupied by environmentalists for over a year, climaxing with violent clashes with police and the city authorities. Some of the woodland was saved, but the struggle became a symbol for the movement. Today much debate surrounds plans to build a larger stadium for Club Brugge football team in fields outside Bruges, and with it a new shopping centre and business park. Campaigners say that the few remaining wooded areas in Flanders are being eroded at a rate of

Left: the port of Zeebrugge is undergoing major development.

first in Belgium to promote (and sell) chickens to residents to use as living, eating waste disposal units.

Transport

Bruges is a place of pedestrians and cyclists: there are more bikes than cars in the city, and the proportion of bikes is on the rise: 5,200 in 2006, compared to 3,000 cars. Tourist coaches are not allowed to enter Bruges except to drop off luggage at hotels, and motorists are dissuaded from entering the city by tortuous one-way systems, free bus shuttles from car parks to the centre and 'park and bike' schemes. Unlike bike-mad Amsterdam, however, Bruges is not a student town with seemingly kamikaze cyclists bearing down on you from every direction: the population is older and rather more sedate in the saddle.

The push to support sustainable transport is happening right across Flanders. All public sector employees are eligible for a free season ticket for public transport if they agree not to commute by car. Those who cycle or walk to work are eligible for tax deductions relative to the distance they travel each day. There are also, in West Flanders, initiatives to encourage people to go shopping by bike: you collect points for cycling at shops and enter a prize draw. For school pupils, there are growing stretches of safe cycle track separate from the road, in streets around schools, which also organise 'bike pools' for children to ride to school in a chaperoned group.

'I've planted many trees in my life. I believe now that planting and re-planting forests is the most productive cultural activity that one can do.'
(Amedée Visart de Bocarmé, burgomaster of Bruges 1876–1924)
Count Visart de Bocarmé was a pioneer in the creation of parks and green spaces around Bruges. He transformed the city ramparts into the ring canal park; the Visartpark outside the ring is named in his honour.

1 hectare (2½ acres/two football pitches) every 36 days.

Towards the coast, the development of Zeebrugge into a major port has led to factories, warehouses and roads encroaching on the historic villages of Lissewege and Dudzele. However, development around the port is restricted, in an official bird protection zone, which has been recognised as an internationally important breeding area for species including the Little Tern, Common Tern and Sandwich Tern.

Recycling

Lots of tourists mean heaps of restaurant waste, so in Bruges, all restaurants have to separate food waste for composting. Flanders claims to be the world champion for separating and recycling waste. In 2006, over 70 percent of domestic waste collected had been separated. Of the 531kg of waste that each inhabitant produces per year, just 153kg is not recycled, and must be incinerated (there is no landfill in Flanders). A strong carrot-and-stick policy has led to this: the requisite bin-bags for roadside collection of non-recyclable waste cost €1–1.50 each, to cover the cost of incineration – bags for recyclable tins, cans, plastic bottles and cartons are very cheap, and paper and cardboard can be bundled with string and left in a cardboard box for collection.

One-third of Flemish families also do home-composting (garden waste is collected). The province of West Flanders, of which Bruges is the capital, was the

Essentials

B ruges is small, compact and among the easi-est of European cities to negotiate. The locals are open, helpful and friendly, and most speak very good English. This section contains all the practical information that you may need during your trip or before departing. It describes how to understand postcodes, use the phone, where to go to check your e-mail and what to do in an emergency or if you fall ill. It gives approximate currency conversions to use as a guide and tourist office information. It also lists the public holidays in Belgium, when museums, shops and many restaurants will be closed.

Embassies/Consulates

Australia
Rue Guimard 6, 1040 Brussels; tel: 02 286 05 00
Canada
Avenue de Tervuren 2, 1040 Brussels; tel: 02 741 06 11
New Zealand
Square de Meeus 1, 1000 Brussels; tel: 02 512 10 40
Republic of Ireland
Chaussée d'Etterbeek 180, 1040 Brussels; tel: 02 235 66 76
South Africa
Rue Montoyer 17–19, 1040 Brussels; tel: 02 285 44 00
UK
Rue d'Arlon 85, 1040 Brussels; tel: 02 287 62 11
US
Boulevard du Régent 27, 1000 Brussels; tel: 02 508 21 11

Emergencies

Ambulance, Fire: 100
Police: 101
Pan-European emergency number: 112

Health

EU NATIONALS
EU nationals who fall ill in Belgium are eligible to receive emergency treatment. You will have to pay, but are

entitled to claim back 75 per-cent of the cost of seeing a doctor or dentist and of pre-scription drugs. You will have to pay part of the costs of hospital treatment. Ambu-lance travel is not covered.

To receive a refund you need a European Health Insurance Card. For UK citi-zens, these are available online at www.dh.gov.uk, by picking up a form in a post office or by phoning: 0845 606 2030. Reimbursements are handled in Belgium by Sickness Funds Offices (Mutualité/Ziekenfonds).

NORTH AMERICANS
International Association for Medical Assistance to Travellers (IAMAT), 2162 Gordon Street, Guelph, Ontario N1L 1G6, Canada; tel: 519 836 0102; www.iamat.org This non-profit group offers members fixed rates for medical treatment. Members receive a medical record completed by their doctor and a directory of English-speaking IAMAT doctors who are on call 24 hours a day. Membership is free but donations are appreciated.

Metric to Imperial Conversions
Metres-Feet 1 = 3.28
Kilometres-Miles 1 = 0.62
Hectares-Acres 1 = 2.47
Kilos-Pounds 1 = 2.2

HOSPITALS
AZ Sint-Jan
Ruddershove 10; tel: 050 45 21 11; www.azbrugge.be; bus: 13

PHARMACIES
For details of duty pharma-cies *(apotheeke)* open at night, check notices in any pharmacy window or call 0900 10 500 (8.30–10pm) or 050 44 88 44 (10pm–9am). Pharmacies are identifiable by a green neon cross sign.

Internet

Many hotels offer e-mail facil-ities. Internet cafés include:
Bauhaus
Langestraat 135; tel: 050 34 10 93; www.bauhaus.be; bus: 6, 16; map p.133 E1
Bean Around the World
Genthof 5; tel: 050 70 35 72; bus: 4, 14; map p.132 C1
Snuffel Backpackers Hostel
Ezelstraat 47; tel: 050 33 31 33;

Left: a pharmacy.

enquiries, tel: 1405 (international: 1304). For online information: www.infobel.be.

Time

Belgium is GMT+1 hour (+2 Apr–end Oct). When it is noon in Bruges, it is 6am in New York, 10pm in Sydney.

Tourist information

IN BRUGES
In&Uit
Concertgebouw building; 't Zand 34; tel: 050 44 46 46; www.bruges.be/toerisme; daily 10am–6pm; bus: 0/Centrum; map p.134 B3

UK

Tourism Flanders-Brussels
Flanders House, 1a Cavendish Square, London W1G 0LD; tel: 0207 307 7730; www.visit flanders.co.uk
Belgian Tourist Offiice Brussels and Wallonia
217 Marsh Wall, London E14 9FJ; tel: 0207 537 1132; www.belgiumtheplaceto.be

US

Belgian Tourist Offiice
220 East 42nd Street, Suite 3402, New York, NY 10017; tel: 212 758 8130; www.visitbelgium.com

Visas

EU nationals require a valid personal identity card or passport to visit Belgium. Other visitors require a valid passport. No visa is required for visitors from the EU, US, Canada, Australia, New Zealand, South Africa or Japan. Nationals of other countries may need a visa. If in doubt (and if visiting for over 90 days), check www.diplomatie.be or with the Belgian embassy in your home country. Everyone over the age of 12 must carry a personal identity card or passport at all times.

www.snuffel.be; bus: 3, 13; map p.132 B1
Teleboetiek
Corner of Langestraat-Predikherenstraat; tel: 050 34 74 72; bus: 6, 16; map p.135 D4

Money

Belgium uses euros (€), divided into 100 cents. Bank notes come in 5, 10, 20, 50, 100, 200 and 500 euros. The approximate exchange rate is £1 to €1.5 and US$1 to 0.7 euros. There are plenty of ATMs in the city. Most shops, restaurants and hotels accept credit cards, but few cafés or bars do.

Post

Bruges Central Post Offiice
Markt 5; tel: 050 47 13 12; www.post.be; Mon–Fri 9am–6pm, Sat 9am–3pm; map p.134 C4; see website for other branches. Mail boxes are red. Buy stamps from post offices and shops selling postcards.

Public holidays

1 January New Year's Day
1 May Labour Day
21 July National Day
15 August Assumption
1 November All Saints' Day
11 November Armistice Day
25 December Christmas Day
Moveable holidays include Easter Monday, Ascension Day and Whit Monday. Holidays falling on a weekend are taken the following Monday.

Telephones

Fixed-line telephone numbers in Bruges start 050. You need to use the area code. The code for Belgium is +32. When dialling from abroad, omit the first 0 of the code. For English-speaking directory

Below: a Bruges postbox.

Food and Drink

Belgians know how to get the best out of their land (and sea) and onto their plates, from the game-based dishes of the Ardennes and white asparagus around Mechelen, to the eels, shrimps and Ostend sole of the North Sea coast, behind the dunes of which graze herds of 'Belgian blue' beef cows. The locals are proud of producing the world's best beer, chocolate, and chips, but not ashamed that their 'national dish', mussels, comes mainly from the sea off the Netherlands. Bruges has an enormous variety of restaurants, although a large number are geared towards tourists. That said, it is hard to eat badly in Belgium.

Belgian Cuisine

Not a lot has changed in Belgian attitudes towards eating and drinking since the days of medieval banquets and Brueghelian feasts: the local cuisine may not be widely known, but Belgians have a hearty taste for good food, enjoyed with cheery company in comfortable surroundings, and washed down

Below: prawns washed down with a Belgian beer.

with a few glasses of beer or (usually French) wine.

There are two main regional cuisines: Flemish and Walloon. The former features plenty of fish, eels, chicken and vegetables, the latter is rich in game and mushrooms. Brussels is famous for its *stoemp* (mash with different vegetables), served with sausage), meatballs in tomato sauce and Brussels sprouts.

It is often reported that Belgium has more Michelin-starred restaurants per capita than France, and there is a trend in pricier restaurants for 'tasting menus' – lots of courses, small portions and showy presentation of unidentifiable ingredients – but most restaurants prefer to remain informal and family-friendly. Typical dishes include:

Waterzooï – a Ghent stew of fish, potatoes, carrots, onions and more in a thin, creamy soup-like sauce. More commonly made with chicken these days, which is cheaper.

Mosselen-frieten (moules-frites) – the classic dish of mussels and chips:

mussels (bred in Zeeland, the Netherlands) are served in a large black casserole dish in a thin stock of celery and onion (plus possibly white wine, garlic, or other variation on the theme). Chips are served on the side, with mayonnaise. The price of a kilo of mussels is always of keen interest at the start of the season, in August. In a good year, they will be plump and plentiful. Some restaurants will only serve mussels during the season (a month with an 'r' in its name); others buy in from Spain or elsewhere, although these are generally viewed as an inferior product.

Frietjes (frites) – chips, fried twice for the unique Belgian consistency. Sold out of a roadside van (frietkot) and accompanied with a wide choice of sauces, most with a mayonnaise base.

Gegratineerd witloof – baked Belgian endive wrapped in a slice of ham and baked in the oven in a white sauce topped with cheese.

Garnaalkroketten– shrimp croquettes: a restau-

Left: mussels cooked with celery and onion.

capital of Belgium, home to the world's largest brewer, Inbev (which makes Stella Artois, Hoegaarden, Leffe and Jupiler).

Lambic beers are wild beers, so called because their fermentation involves exposure to wild yeast. Many have a sour, apple-like taste, but fruit may have been added to these to impart a distinctive flavour. Kriek, a lambic beer flavoured with cherries, comes in a round glass, while Frambozen is a pale pink raspberry brew served in a tall stemmed glass.

Gueuze is a type of lambic made by blending very young lambics which are fermented for a second time in a corked bottle (hence its nickname: Brussels Champagne). Gueuze beers have an almost cidery flavour. Boon, Cantillon and the award-winning Oud Beersel breweries produce gueuze varieties.

White beer *(witbier)* is a wheat beer flavoured with coriander and orange peel. Cloudy and generally light and

Even though tap water is perfectly drinkable, regrettably few restaurants in Belgium are happy to serve it with a meal. Belgium's own mineral waters are Spa (the blue label is flat, the red sparkling) and Bru (sparkling).

lemon balm; every chef has his own recipe.

Beer

Beer is to the Belgians what wine is to the French and, indeed, many Belgian beers complete the last stage of their fermentation in corked bottles. Several hundred types are produced, all of which have their distinctive character – and are served in their own, distinctive glass. Leuven is the beer

rant's reputation can stand or fall depending on how they prepare this popular starter. The more of the tiny North Sea shrimps that are combined with bechamel sauce and then deep-fried in breadcrumbs, the better. Served with deep-fried parsley on the side.

Vlaamse stoofkarbonaden (carbonnades flamandes) – thick, rich beef stew, where chunks of meat are cooked for hours in beer.

Maatjes – raw herring, sold on seafood stalls and fishmongers and eaten as they come with chopped raw onions: the Belgian sushi.

Paling in 't groen – eel in green sauce: a subtle dish where the eel is cooked in a mixture of chervil, spinach, parsley, sorrel, tarragon and

Below: in Belgium chips are served with mayonnaise.

youthful in flavour, it often comes with a slice of lemon.

Trappist is a term for beers brewed in an abbey or under the control of Trappist monks. Only six breweries in Belgium (plus one in the Netherlands) bear the authentic Trappist label: Chimay, Orval, Rochefort, Westmalle, Westvleteren, Achelse Kluis. Among their beers, Tripel denotes a very strong beer that was served to the abbot and other important personages; the monks drank the Dubbel, while the peasants (i.e. everyone else) had only a watery version.

Kwak (a strong, light-coloured beer) is served in a glass with a spherical base that sits in a wooden stand in order to remain upright. The 1½-litre glass and its stand are so valuable that customers must often give up a shoe to ensure they do not run off with the merchandise.

One highly acclaimed strong beer (8.5 percent) is **Delirium Tremens**, which can take you by surprise if you are not used to it – though if you see pink elephants, they are on the label and not in your head. Another powerful but delicious beer is **Corsendonck Agnus Dei**.

Bruges has one brewery, the **De Halve Maan**, which produces two beers: the Tripel ale Straffe Hendrik (9 percent) and the gentler Brugse Zot (6 percent), a blond.

SEE ALSO CAFÉS AND BARS, P.30

Genever

The Belgian gin, genever was invented in the Low Countries around 1580, and the juniper-flavoured spirit was discovered by British troops fighting against the Spanish in the Dutch War of Independence. They knocked it back gratefully to give them what became known as 'Dutch courage'. At the beginning of the 19th century, there was a genever brewery and distillery in every town. Today, only a handful remain. Bruges' one specialist genever bar closed a few years ago, although there is still one in Ghent.

The spirit is made by distilling an unfiltered and fermented mash of malted grains – mainly barley – and flavouring it with aromatics such as juniper berries, caraway seeds or fennel. The barley malt gives traditional genever more body and grain flavour than English-style gin, which uses neutral spirits and was developed after 17th-

century Flemish distillers began trading in London.

There are three types of genever: Oude, the old, straw-coloured, pungently sweet style; Jonge, a newer style which tastes cleaner and more delicate; and Korenwijn, which is cask-aged with a high percentage of malted spirit.

Chocolates

Belgium makes some of the best chocolate in the world, and is most famous for its pralines – sculpted shells containing soft fillings, of which a dizzying variety exist. The industry took off in the 1880s, helped by the acquisition of the Congo, which opened up access to Africa's cocoa fields. Every Belgian has their own opinion on who makes the best chocolate and which shop they prefer. On Saturday afternoons, people line up outside

> Belgium is home to the world's largest brewery, now known as AB InBev following a merger with Anheuser-Busch in late 2008. The Leuven-based brewer makes Stella Artois, Hoegaarden, Leffe and Jupiler and has roots that can be traced back to 1366.

Below: rows of flavoured genever, the Belgian gin.

Above: Belgium is famous for its high-quality chocolate.

chocolatiers' windows to purchase a box of mixed pralines (a common gift to a hostess when you are invited to dinner). Sample a variety and then take your own pick.

Food Shops

CHOCOLATE
Van Oost
Wollestraat 11, tel: 050 33 14 54; daily 9.30am–6.30pm; bus: 0/Centrum; map p.134 C4
Arguably the best choc shop in town. The service can be a little frosty but their walnuts coated in chocolate – produced during autumn – are to die for.

Sweertvaegher
Philipstockstraat 29; tel: 050 33 83 67; www.sweertvaegher.be; Tue–Sat 9.30am–6pm; bus: 0/Centrum; map p.134 C4
Tiny little shop that does excellent chocs, including wooden-boxed flocks of Brugsche Swaentjes (Bruges Swans).

Otherwise, the following chains (Leonidas being the cheapest) do a wide selection and are reliable and good:

Galler
Steenstraat 5; tel: 050 61 20 62; www.galler.com, daily 10.30am–6pm; bus: 0/Centrum;

map p.134 C4
Leonidas
at Confiiserie Dalipan, Steenstraat 4; tel: 050 33 40 60; www.leonidas.be; daily 9.30am–6pm, bus: 0/Centrum; map p.134 C4
Neuhaus
Streenstraat 66; tel: 050 33 15 30; www.neuhaus.be; Mon–Fri 10am–6pm, Sat 1.30–6pm; bus: 0/Centrum; map p.134 B4

Drinks

2be – Foodshopping
Wollestraat 53; tel: 050 61 12 22; www.2-be.biz; daily 10am–7pm; bus: 0/Centrum; map p.134 C4
Emporium of Belgian food and drink – from beer to sweets to herbal teas – in a medieval mansion and with a superb view from the bar terrace.

Bacchus Cornelius
Academiestraat 17; tel: 050 34 53 38; www.bacchus cornelius.com; Wed–Mon 10am–6pm; bus: 0/Centrum, 4, 14; map p.132 C1
A good beer selection, including some rarities, and an open fire in winter. They make their own genever too.

De Bier Tempel
Philipstockstraat 7; tel: 050 34 37 30; daily 9.30am–6pm; bus: 0/Centrum; map p.134 C4

Centrally located but not large; under same ownership as nearby beer-brasserie Cambrinus, and with lots of suitable gift items – T-shirts, glasses, greeting cards – for the beer-lover in your life.

The Bottle Shop
Wollestraat 13; tel: 050 34 99 80; www.thebottleshop.eu; Wed–Mon 10am–7pm; bus: 0/Centrum; map p.134 C4
Around 450 ales on offer, including Trappist beers and gift-friendly packs. It also sells Belgian genever in stoneware jars and a wide selection of bottled water.

Further Reading

Everybody Eats Well in Belgium Cookbook by Ruth Van Waerebeek-Gonzalez and Maria Robbins, illustrated by Melissa Sweet, Workman Publishing (1996). A lovingly detailed cookbook.

Michael Jackson's Great Beers of Belgium, 6th edition, Brewers Publications (2008). The late beer expert drank his way devotedly through the beer rosters of many a land. He came away from Belgium convinced that it has one of the world's greatest beer-brewing traditions.

History

c.1000–800 BC
Celtic tribes settle in what is now Flanders.

1ST CENTURY BC
Celtic farmers are established on the coastal plain around what is now Bruges.

57 BC

Julius Caesar's invading Roman legions defeat the Belgae, a conglomeration of Celtic tribes, in the northern part of Gaul (today's France).

1ST CENTURY AD
A Gallo-Roman settlement is founded beside the Rivers Reie and Dijver, on the site of present-day Bruges, and maintains trading links with Britain and Gaul.

4TH–6TH CENTURY
The Franks, a Germanic people, cross the Rhine and settle between the rivers Meuse and Schelde.

498
Conversion to Christianity of Frankish King Clovis.

8TH CENTURY
Foundation of Ghent abbeys; St Eloy writes of the municipium Flandrense, an important town in the Flemish coastal plain, which seems likely to have been Bruges.

768
Charlemagne's unified kingdom is established.

800
Charlemagne, King of the Franks, is crowned Emperor of the West.

814
Death of Charlemagne and division of empire.

843
The Frankish Empire splits into three. Flanders west of the Schelde joins West Francia; the territory east of the Schelde becomes part of the Middle Kingdom, then, in 855, of Lotharingia (Lorraine).

c.850
A fort is built in the town for defence against attacks by Viking raiders.

861
Baldwin Iron Arm elopes with the daughter of Carolingian King Charles the Bald.

863
Baldwin becomes first Count of Flanders and occupies the Burg castle in Bruges.

864
The first record of the name 'Bruggia – a melding of the Old Norse bryggja (jetty) and Rugja, the original name of the River Reie – appears on coins of Charles the Bald.

c.940
Count Arnulf I develops the Burg, building his castle and the Church of St Donatian there.

c.1040
An English text calls Bruges an important maritime trading centre, but by the end of the century access to the sea is closed by silting.

1127
Count Charles the Good is murdered in St Donatian's. Thierry of Alsace becomes Count of Flanders. Bruges is granted its first charter and building of the city wall begins.

1134
Flooding creates a channel, the Zwin, from the sea to Damme. Bruges builds a canal to Damme, reopening a maritime trading route.

1150
Count Thierry of Alsace is said to bring back from the Second Crusade a relic of the Blood of Christ.

1177
Bruges is granted a revised charter by Count Philip of Alsace.

13TH CENTURY
Some of Bruges' most prominent buildings, including the Belfort, Hallen, Begijnhof and Sint-Jans hospitaal are begun.

1250

With a population of 40–50,000, Bruges is among the biggest and richest cities in north-west Europe, through trade and textiles manufacture.

1297

King Philip IV of France annexes Flanders. New fortifications are begun.

1302

Weaver Pieter de Coninck and butcher Jan Breidel foment rebellion against France. French citizens and sympathisers are massacred in the 'Bruges Matins', and an army of Flemish peasants and craftsmen slaughters the French knights at the Battle of the Golden Spurs at Kortrijk.

1305

War with France ends in a treaty unfavourable to Flanders. Bruges' defences are dismantled.

1316

Famine strikes the city, killing thousands; 33 years later thousands more lives are lost in a plague.

1376

Building of the Town Hall begins, at a time of great prosperity from international trade.

1384

Count Louis is succeeded by his daughter Margaret, wife of Philip the Bold, Duke of Burgundy. Flanders becomes part of Burgundian kingdom. The dazzling Burgundian century begins.

15TH CENTURY

Cloth-making declines, but prosperity continues from trade and banking.

1419

Philip the Good of Burgundy made Duke of Flanders.

1430

Duke Philip the Good founds the Order of the Golden Fleece in Bruges.

1436

Jan van Eyck paints the Virgin and Child.

1436–8

Philip the Good cruelly crushes a rebellion against him in Bruges.

1474–9

Hans Memling paints the Triptych of St John.

1477

Death of Duke Charles the Bold sparks another rebellion. His successor is Mary of Burgundy, wife of Habsburg Crown Prince Maximilian of Austria. She grants the city a new charter.

1482

After Mary's death in a riding accident, the Habsburg reign begins, with Maximilian of Austria. Bruges rebelsagainst its new rulers, imprisoning Maximilian in the Craenenburg mansion. When freed, he moves the ducal residence to Ghent.

1520

Silting of the Zwin closes Bruges' access to the sea. Economic decline begins.

1527

Bruges' first Protestant martyr is burned at the stake in the Burg.

1541

Mercator draws first map of Flanders.

1555

Charles V abdicates in favour of his son, King Philip II of Spain.

1559

The Bishopric of Bruges is established.

1566

Protestant 'Iconoclasts' sack churches across the Low Countries.

61

1567–79

Religious wars in the southern Low Countries.

1577

Bruges hesitantly joins the Low Countries' rebellion against Spanish rule.

1580

The city signs the Treaty of Utrecht against Spain; Protestantism becomes the only permitted religion.

1584

Spain re-establishes control. Many Protestant merchants, artists and craftsmen flee to Holland. The following year the Scheldt estuary is blockaded and Bruges goes into steep decline.

1622

Opening of a canal to Ostend gives Bruges an outlet to the sea again.

1701–14

War of the Spanish Succession.

1715

By the Treaty of Utrecht, Belgium passes under the authority of the Austrian Holy Roman Emperor Charles VI.

1744–8

Bruges is occupied by the French.

1753

The Coupure Canal opened, allowing sea-going vessels into the city centre.

1780

Maria Theresa dies; Joseph II accedes.

1789–90

Pro-French revolutionaries proclaim the short-lived 'United States of Belgium'; the Austrian Army regains control.

1794–5

Revolutionary France invades and occupies the city. Many churches and monasteries are destroyed. French occupy the country for 20 years.

1815

Napoleon defeated at Waterloo. Bruges becomes part of the Kingdom of the Netherlands under William I of Orange.

1830

Bruges joins the Southern Netherlands' revolt against Dutch rule, resulting in the formation of the Kingdom of Belgium, under King Leopold I.

1838

Railway connecting Brussels, Ghent, Bruges and Ostend opens.

1847

Hunger riots erupt in Bruges, the poorest city in Belgium.

1892

Georges Rodenbach's novel *Bruges-la-Morte* is published.

1892

The Flemish poet Guido Gezelle dies in the city.

1904

Work on the new Bruges sea harbour, Zeebrugge, is completed.

1914–18

World War I. Germans invade neutral Belgium and occupy Bruges for four years, destroying Zeebrugge harbour as they retreat. Battles around Ieper (Ypres) and along River Ijzer are among the war's bloodiest.

1940–44

World War II. Germans occupy Bruges for 4 years, again destroying Zeebrugge harbour as they retreat. The government is in exile in London.

1948

Customs union between Belgium, the Netherlands and Luxembourg (Benelux).

1949

Belgium joins NATO.

1950

Modern tourist boom begins.

1951

King Baudouin I ascends the throne after the abdication of Leopold III.

1957

Belgium is a founder member of the European Economic Community, the forerunner of today's European Union.

1971

Bruges merges with surrounding municipalities, making it Flanders' third biggest city. Flemish and Walloon communities are given greater autonomy in cultural affairs; a process extended in 1980.

1977

Prime minister Leo Tindemans establishes three federal regions in Belgium: Flanders, Wallonia and Brussels. Bruges city centre is made virtually car-free.

1984

Flanders adopts bilingual Brussels as its regional capital.

1989

Regional governments created.

1993

King Baudouin I dies and is succeeded by his brother Albert II.

1994

A new constitution completes Belgium's transition to a federal state, with considerable powers devolved to regions.

2002

Bruges is European City of Culture for a year; the Concertgebouw concert hall opens. Euro becomes Belgium's currency.

2008

Flemish Christian Democrat Herman Van Rompuy becomes prime minister after predecessor Yves Leterme (below) resigns over a banking scandal.

2009

Regional elections for the Flemish government result in a three-party coalition of Christian Democrats, Socialists and Flemish Nationalists. Yves Leterme returns for a second term in office after Van Rompuy takes up the post of President of the European Council.

Hotels

A small city with few corporate travellers, Bruges has been spared the plague of dreary chain hotels that blights many a destination. At the same time, there are few large, grand hotels. Most occupy historic properties in the city centre, with rooms decorated in romantic, English country house style or, increasingly, a more contemporary Flemish aesthetic. Be warned that room sizes and features can vary considerably within the same establishment, and expect to pay more for a canal view. There are also a growing number of bed and breakfast places in tastefully renovated homes in the heart of Bruges.

Markt and Burg

Crowne Plaza Brugge
Burg 10; tel: 050 44 68 44; www.crowneplaza.com/brugge bel; €–€€€; bus: 0/Centrum; map p.134 C4
This modern block is an eyesore on the historic Burg square. Inside, however, you get the fabulous view out, capacious beds and the details and service you would expect from a top-flight hotel. The basement contains the ruins of St Donatian's, the former cathedral, which make for a bizarre feature in a conference suite. Low-season room rates can be excellent.

Martin's Orangerie
Karthuizerinnenstraat 10; tel: 050 34 16 49; www.martins-hotels.com; €€€; bus: 0/Centrum; map p.134 C3
A firm favourite with visiting celebrities, the Orangerie occupies a charming 15th-century convent with water lapping the walls. Located in a narrow street close to the belfry, it could not be more central. A recent stylish makeover has transformed it into a chic boutique hotel furnished with fine antiques. There is a lakeside terrace and a romantic orangerie. Try to avoid ground-floor rooms facing the street.

The Pand
Pandreitje 16; tel: 050 34 06 66; www.pandhotel.com; €€€€; bus: 6, 16; map p.135 C3

Below: a superior 'pergola' room at De Swaene hotel.

Price ranges, which are given as a guide only, are for a standard double room with bathroom, including service, tax and usually breakfast (pricier establishments will charge an extra €15–30):
€ under €85
€€ €85–125
€€€ €125–180
€€€€ over €180

64

Left: Martin's Orangerie is right by the water.

For longer stays, you might consider booking a self-catering flat or house. This is often much cheaper than a hotel, especially as you can eat at home. The minimum stay is usually two days. The tourist office recommends 50 owners of rental properties on its website. Most properties can be booked online through their own websites.

Die Swaene
Steenhouwersdijk 1; tel: 050 34 27 98; fax: 050 33 66 74; www.dieswaene.com; €€€; bus: 6, 16; map p.135 C4

Most people fall in love with this lovely brick hotel by a quiet, tree-lined canal. The main building, a former tailors' guildhouse, has old wooden staircases and heavy oak furniture. The 'Pergola' extension, a historic former warehouse across the canal, is decorated in luxurious modern style. The 30 rooms come in different sizes and styles, some of them with elegant four-poster beds, some – the downstairs rooms – rather dark and pokey. There

A boutique hotel with 26 rooms in a converted 18th-century carriage house close to the picturesque Rozenhoedkaai. Owned by antique dealers, it is brimming with cachet and the bedrooms are all individually styled.

Relais Bourgondisch Cruyce
Wollestraat 41–47; tel: 050 33 79 26; www.relaisbourgondisch cruyce.be; €€€€; bus: 1, 11, 6, 16; map p.135 C4

A gorgeous small hotel in two gabled houses with timbered facades backing onto a canal and facing a pretty, off-street courtyard. Decorated in sumptuous 17th-century Flemish style with carved furniture, stone floors and large fireplaces, it featured in hit film *In Bruges*. The 16 bedrooms are individually designed, combining traditional decor with a hint of modern design. Get a room with a canal view if you can.

Below: the clean and cosy breakfast room at The Pand.

The local phone numbers given in this guide include the Bruges area code '050'. When dialling from abroad, omit the first 0 of the code.

is a pool and sauna and a Romeo and Juliet package aimed at honeymooners.

South

Boat-Hotel De Barge

Bargeweg 15; tel: 050 38 51 50; www.hoteldebarge.be; €€€; bus: 2, 12

Wake up to the sound of ducks outside the window in this unusual hotel located in a converted Flemish canal barge. The rooms may be small, but they have an appealing nautical flavour, with white wood, blue paint and bright red lifejackets laid out on the beds. The hotel has a bar, terrace, restaurant and car park. Located just outside the old town, a brisk 10-min walk from the centre.

Botaniek

Waalsestraat 23; tel: 050 34 14 24; www.botaniek.be; €€; bus: 6, 16; map p.135 D4

A simple, friendly hotel located in a quiet street close to the Astridpark. The nine-room establishment occupies an 18th-century town house furnished in traditional, Louis XV style. Top-floor rooms have wonderful views of gabled houses and ancient spires.

Egmond

Minnewater 15; tel: 050 34 14 45; www.egmond.be; €€; bus:

2, 20, 21; map p.134 C1

This attractive, small hotel is located in a gabled Flemish mansion next to the romantic Minnewater lake. The interior is furnished in an appealing Flemish traditional style, complete with tiled floors, oak chests and 18th-century fireplaces. The eight bedrooms look out on a rambling garden, making for peaceful nights. There is a car park for guests, and the station is just a 10-min walk away.

Jan Brito

Freren Fonteinstraat 1; tel: 050 33 06 01; www.janbrito.eu; €€€; bus: 6, 16; map p.135 D4

A real gem in the heart of Bruges but away from the bustle, this 36-room hotel occupies a 16th-century merchant's house and 18th-century rear building with a secluded Renaissance garden. Tastefully decorated, with marble fireplaces, thick carpets and an oak staircase.

't Keizershof

Oostmeers 126; tel: 050 33 87 28; www.hotelkeizershof.be; €; bus: 0/Centrum; map p.134 B1

The perfect place for anyone travelling on a tight budget,

Below: De Tuilerieen's beautifully designed interior.

Above: the grandly styled breakfast room at the Jan Brito hotel.

this compact, seven-room establishment is located in a pretty street close to the railway station. The rooms are as cheap as they come, yet they are clean and comfortable; each has a sink, while WC and shower are shared. A notice at the entrance sums up the owner's outlook: 'When you are sleeping, we look just like one of those big fancy hotels.' Free parking.

Montanus
Nieuwe Gentweg 78; tel: 050 33 11 76; www.montanus.be; €€; bus: 1, 11; map p.135 C3
Tasteful, restrained elegance in a historic house, once the home of one of Belgium's most famous statesmen. In addition to the main house, there are colonial-style pavilion rooms in the serene private garden, and these are cheaper. Of the 20 rooms, one is suitable for disabled guests.

De Tuilerieen
Dijver 7; tel: 050 34 36 91; www.hoteltuilerieen.com; €€€€; bus: 0/Centrum; map p.134 C3
The most luxurious hotel in town: a 45-room pale pink mansion facing the main canal. With courteous staff and antique-stuffed rooms, this hotel is hard to resist. Some rooms have views of the canal, while others face the garden. There is also a bright swimming pool, sauna and steam room. Breakfast is expensive; you may prefer to order coffee and croissants in a nearby patisserie.

West

Ensor
Speelmansrei 10; tel: 050 34 25 89; www.ensorhotel.be; €; bus: 0/Centrum; map p.134 A4
This friendly 12-room hotel occupies a brick building on a quiet canal near the 't Zand. The rooms are plainly furnished, but well-maintained, and all have en-suite bathrooms, making this one of the best budget hotels in the city.

Karel De Stoute
Moerstraat 23; tel: 050 34 33 17; www.hotelkareldestoute.be; €–€€; bus: 0/Centrum, 12; map p.134 B4
Named after 15th-century Duke of Burgundy Charles the Bold, this charming hotel occupies a building that once formed part of the Prinsenhof ducal residence. Run by a friendly couple, the nine-room hotel offers a relaxed atmosphere in the heart of the old town. The rooms are tastefully furnished, and priced according to size. Some have oak beams, while two have bathrooms located in a 15th century circular staircase tower. The bar is in an ancient cellar with a vaulted brick ceiling. There is also free internet access.

Kempinski Hotel Dukes' Palace
Prinsenhof 8; tel: 050 44 78 88;

Price ranges, which are given as a guide only, are for a standard double room with bathroom, including service, tax and usually breakfast (pricier establishments will charge an extra €15–30):

€	under €85
€€	€85–125
€€€	€125–180
€€€€	over €180

Above: not all hotels offer breakfast, so check before booking.

There are a growing number of bed and breakfasts *(gasthuizen)* in and around Bruges. These are located in private homes – including an improbably grand neo-Gothic castle just outside the city – and offer an inexpensive alternative to hotels. Many are owned by local artists, architects and designers, and some have stunning interiors and gardens. The owners are nearly always ready to provide you with insider advice on the best restaurants and cafés in the area. To locate a B&B, visit the Bruges Guild of Guest Houses website, which lists 44 approved addresses (www.brugge-bedand breakfast.com), or the city tourist office, www.brugge.be. Bookings can normally be made online. Be aware that most owners do not accept credit cards.

www.kempinski-bruges.com; €€€€; bus: 0/Centrum; map p.134 B4

An exclusive choice: this hotel was opened in 2008 in the neo-Gothic Prinsenhof, a 19th-century rebuild of the Medieval Princes' Court created by Burgundian Duke Philip the Good in 1429. The 93 rooms, pool, banqueting suite and spa ensure 21st-century standards of luxury; the listed chapel and other details uphold the building's rich history.

Prinsenhof

Ontvangersstraat 9; tel: 050 34 26 90; www.prinsenhof.be; €€€; bus: 0/Centrum; map p.134 B4

This elegant small hotel around the corner from the former Prinsenhof building (now Kempinski Hotel Dukes' Palace) is traditionally furnished, with wood panelling, chandeliers, and other antiques; it also has excellent bathrooms. There is a warm atmosphere, and the staff are very friendly. 19 rooms.

North

Aragon

Naaldenstraat 22; tel: 050 33 33; www.aragon.be; €€€; bus: 0/Centrum; map p.132 B1

This well-run hotel is located in the heart of the old merchant's quarter, opposite a palace once owned by the Italian Medici family. The 42 rooms were recently renovated in a comfortable English country-house style.

Asiris

Lange Raamstraat 9; tel: 050 34 17 24; www.hotelasiris.be; €; bus: 4, 14; map p.132 C2

A small, family-run hotel in a quiet quarter close to the lovely Sint-Gilliskerk. The 13 bedrooms are furnished in a plain, modern style aimed at travellers on a budget and families. The rooms under the eaves are a tight squeeze and are cheapest. Breakfast is included in the price, making this one of the best inexpensive hotels in town.

Bryghia

Oosterlingenplein 4; tel: 050 33 80 59; www.bryghiahotel.be; €€; bus: 4, 14; map p.132 C1

This friendly, family-run hotel is situated in one of Bruges' most peaceful neighbourhoods, rarely visited by tourists. Part of the 18-room hotel occupies a 15th-century building that once belonged to Hanseatic merchants. The interior is quite cosy and tastefully furnished with comfortable sofas and exposed wood beams. Some rooms enjoy a view of a sleepy canal.

Cavalier

Kuipersstraat 25; tel: 050 33 02 07; www.hotelcavalier.be; €; bus: 0/Centrum; map p.132 B1

In spite of its slightly ramshackle external appearance, this small hotel behind the city theatre is friendly and ordered and provides good value for the cheaper range of hotels. 8 rooms.

Martin's Relais Oud-Huis Amsterdam
Spiegelrei 3; tel: 050 34 18 10; www.martinshotels.com; €€; bus: 4, 14; map p.133 C1
Overlooking a quiet canal in the heart of the old merchants' quarter and near the Markt, this romantic 44-room hotel, set in a 17th-century trading house, has a wooden staircase, chandeliers, beams and antique furniture. There is also a pretty interior courtyard. Skip the hotel breakfast, which costs extra, and walk 5 mins to Het Dagelijks Brood (Philipstockstraat 21) to enjoy coffee and delicious croissants in a typical French farmhouse interior.

Snuffel Backpacker Hostel
Ezelstraat 47–49; tel: 050 33 31 33; www.snuffel.be; €; bus: 3, 13; map p.132 B1
A simple youth hostel with pine bunks in rooms sleeping 4 to 12 people (the small rooms can also be booked as private rooms for two people). Located in a traditional gabled house, it has a ground-floor bar with English newspapers, internet access, its own 'Snuffel' beer and

free live gigs every first and third Saturday of the month, except July and August.

Ter Brughe
Oost-Gistelhof 2; tel: 050 34 03 24; www.hotelterbrughe.com; €€; bus: 4, 14; map p.132 C1
Attractive hotel in the elegant St Giles quarter, 5 mins' walk from the centre of Bruges. Breakfast is served in the 14th-century beamed and vaulted cellar, which was once a warehouse for goods brought along the canal. The 46 rooms are comfortable, if rather faded.

Ter Duinen
Langerei 52; tel: 050 33 04 37; www.hotelterduinen.eu; €€–€€€; bus: 4, 14; map p.132 D3
A little out of centre, 'The Dunes' takes its name from the former abbey across the canal. The conservatory and formal garden are stylish; the rooms are neutrally decorated and pleasant. The cobbled Langerei is quiet at night and windows are super-insulated. Air-conditioning in all rooms.

Ter Reien
Langestraat 1; tel: 050 34 91 00; www.hotelterreien.be; €€; bus: 6, 16; map p.135 D4
As its name suggests, the 'hotel on the canal' is located

Price ranges, which are given as a guide only, are for a standard double room with bathroom, including service, tax and usually breakfast (pricier establishments will charge an extra €15–30):

€	under €85
€€	€85–125
€€€	€125–180
€€€€	over €180

along one of the many beautiful canals in the city. Notably, it occupies the house where the Symbolist painter Fernand Khnopff spent his childhood. The 26 rooms are bright and comfortable. There is a breakfast courtyard.

Walburg
Boomgaardstraat 13–15; tel: 050 34 94 14; www.hotelwalburg.be; €€€€; bus: 6, 16; map p.133 D1
Spacious, elegant hotel in fine, recently restored historic mansion just 100 metres from the Burg. All rooms are larger than average for the city and have Italian marble bathrooms; high ceilings and elaborate cornices abound. 19 rooms.

East

Adornes
St Annarei 26; tel: 050 34 13 36; www.adornes.be; €€€; bus: 4, 14; map p.133 D1
This pretty little 20-room hotel occupies a row of traditional brick houses beside a peaceful canal in the charming St Anna quarter. The rooms are comfortable and bright, some with oak beams. Breakfast is included in the price of the room. There are free bikes for guests' use as well as a limited number of free parking spaces. All Adornes guests receive an advantage card to enjoy special entrance prices to museums and boat trips.

Bauhaus
Langestraat 135–137; tel: 050 34 10 93; www.bauhaus.be; €;

Below: the Walburg's gleaming white restaurant.

Above: the traditional Adornes hotel, as seen from the outside and in.

bus: 6, 16; map p.133 E1
Large budget hotel and youth
hostel offering a variety of
cheap accommodation: en-
suite rooms with shower and
toilet, well-appointed flats for
2–12 people, and dorms with
up to eight beds. There is
bike rental, a cybercafé and a
bar, which, given the meagre
nightlife offerings in Bruges,
is lively and sociable.

Rosenburg
Coupure 30; tel: 050 34 01 94;
www.rosenburg.be; €€; bus: 6,
16; map p.135 D3
A quiet hotel situated on the
banks of a canal approxi-
mately a 10-min walk from the
centre of Bruges. The atmosphere in this modern brick

> Price ranges, which are given
> as a guide only, are for a
> standard double room with
> bathroom, including service,
> tax and usually breakfast
> (pricier establishments will
> charge an extra €15–30):
>
> | | |
> |---|---|
> | € | under €85 |
> | €€ | €85–125 |
> | €€€ | €125–180 |
> | €€€€ | over €180 |

building is relaxed and friendly,
staff are particularly helpful,
and there are good business
facilities. The 27 rooms are
larger than average for the city.

Around

DAMME
Leonardo
Chartreuseweg 20; tel: 050 40 21
40; www.leonardo-hotels.com;
€€; bus: 7, 74; map p.139 C3
Out-of-town option between
the motorway and the centre
with good amenities, an outdoor pool with children's play
area, and easy parking.

De Speye
Damse vaart zuid 5-6; tel: 050
54 85 42; www.hoteldes
peye.be; €; boat or bike to
Damme; map p.139 C3
Small five-room country hotel
in an old building with modern rooms, beside the canal
to Bruges.

Vissershof
Damse vaart noord 44, Hoeke-
Damme; tel: 0475 29 95 29;
www.vissershof.com; €€; train
to Knokke (arrange pick-up from
proprietor); map p.139 C3
Guest house beside the
canal rather further from

Bruges than Damme, with
good access to the coast at
Knokke. Its three rooms are
decorated in delightful style
by photographer Jeep Novak
and his wife Catherine, who
also prepare meals for their
guests. Choose between the
romantic 'white', exotic 'eth-
nic' and cottagey 'pink'
rooms, all very contemporary
with bare floorboards and
carefully selected acces-
sories. Bikes available on
loan. No credit cards.

GHENT
Boatel
Voorhoutkaai 44; tel: 09 267 10
30; www.theboatel.com; €€;
train to Gent-Dampoort; map
p.137 D3
Ghent's first floating hotel
caused a stir when it opened
a few years ago. Located in
the Portus Ganda, a new city
marina, this former 1951 canal
barge has been converted
into an unusual hotel. It has
five small rooms with porthole
windows located in the former
cargo hold and two more
roomy suites on the upper
deck. A 10-min walk to town.

Chambre Plus

Hoogpoort 31; tel: 09 225 37 75; www.chambreplus.be; €€; tram 1 (Sint-Niklaasstraat); map p.137 E2

Homeowner Mia Ackaert has created three sublime Bed and Breakfast rooms in the rear of her family's 18th-century mansion. Ask for the Sultan Room for a wildly romantic decor inspired by the Middle East, or pick the Congo Room to sleep amid jungle-print fabrics. But the best (and most expensive) choice is the Côté Sud, a separate apartment decorated in Mediterranean style, with a lounge, an open fire and a Jacuzzi where you can take a bath under the night sky. A delicious breakfast is included in the price.

Ghent River Hotel

Waaistraat 5; tel: 09 266 10 10; www.ghent-river-hotel.be; €€€€; tram 1 (Gravensteen); map p.136 C4

This waterfront hotel near the Vrijdagmarkt evokes the trading history of Ghent. Some rooms occupy a restored 19th-century sugar factory, while others are in a 16th-century town house; the square was the site of a yarn market in the Middle Ages and the 19th century. When booking, ask for one of the rooms in the former factory, as these have oak beams, brick walls and odd industrial implements used for decoration. The rooms in the modern extension are plainer. The hotel has a rooftop breakfast room with striking views of the old city, a jetty and a fitness room.

Gravensteen

Jan Breydelstraat 35; tel: 09 225 11 50; www.gravensteen.be; €€€; tram 1 (Gravensteen); map p.137 B4

This 19th-century mansion, once the home of an industrial magnate, has been turned into one of the city's most elegant hotels. It is situated across the water from Gravensteen Castle, of which rooms at the front have a fine view, and it has been tastefully renovated and extended. Fitness room and sauna. Disabled access. 46 rooms.

Marriott Ghent Hotel

Drabstraat; tel: 09 233 93 93; www.marriott.com; €€€; tram: 1 (Korenmarkt); map p.137 B4

An enviable location near all the sights and the upmarket chain's high standards have firmly established this newcomer. Part of the hotel fronts on Korenlei, facing the lovely Graslei and looking down to St Nicholas Bridge. Rooms are very comfortable though few have canal views. There is parking beneath the hotel.

The Coast

DE HAAN

Auberge des Rois

Zeedijk 1; tel: 059 23 30 18; www.beachhotel.be; €€; coast tram (De Haan aan Zee); map p.138 B4

Fine modern hotel on the beach, built in De Haan's *belle-époque*-villa style.

Belle Epoque

Leopoldlaan 5; tel: 059 23 34 65; www.hotelbelleepoque.be; €€; coast tram (De Haan aan Zee); map p.138 B4

A grand old villa given a modern makeover, and converted into a notable hotel with modern facilities, and close to the beach.

Grand Hôtel Belle Vue

Koninklijk Plein 5; tel: 059 23 34 39; www.hotelbellevue.be; €€; coast tram (De Haan aan Zee); map p.138 B4

A more traditional old villa, this superb and rather fanciful-looking domed hotel is close to the stop for the Coast Tram.

OSTEND

Hotel du Parc

Marie-Joseplein 3; tel: 059 70 16 80; www.hotelduparc.be; €€; bus: 5 from station to Marie-Joséplein; map p.138 B3

A rare surviving pre-war building in Ostend, this Art Deco hotel behind the casino and the promenade has a wealth of stylish, original fittings in the bar-brasserie on the street. Get a room at the front; those at the rear can be pokey.

Below: the Hôtel Belle Vue has seen many prestigious guests.

Language

The people of Flanders speak Dutch. Behind this simple statement lies a thicket of complication. There is no such language – the word reflects the historical English inability to distinguish between the languages of Germany (Deutsch) and the Low Countries (Nederlands), and their lumping of them together and corrupting it to Dutch. The language academy of Flanders calls its language 'Netherlandic', but is willing to live with Dutch as an internationally accepted substitute. If this is far too complicated, most people in Bruges are happy to speak English or German (but not necessarily French).

General

Yes *Ja*
No *Nee*
Please *Alstublieft*
Thank you (very much) *Dank u (wel)*
Excuse me *Excuseer/pardon*
Hello *Dag/Hallo*
Goodbye *Dag/tot ziens*
Good morning *Goedemorgen*
Good afternoon *Goedemiddag*
Good evening *Goedenavond*
Do you speak English? *Spreekt u Engels?*
I don't understand *Ik begrijp het niet*
I am sorry *Het spijt me/Sorry*
No problem *Geen probleem*
Can you help me? *Kunt u mij helpen?*
What is your name? *Wat is uw naam?/Hoe heet u?*
My name is... *Ik heet...*
I am English/American *Ik ben Engelsman/Engelse/Amerikaan*
When? *Wanneer?*
At what time? *Hoe laat?*
What time is it? *Hoe laat is het?*
today *vandaag*
yesterday/tomorrow *gisteren/morgen*
now/later *nu/later*
this morning *vanmorgen*
this afternoon *deze namiddag/vanmiddag*
this evening *vanavond*
day/week *dag/week*
month/year *maand/jaar*
here/there *hier/daar*
left/right *links/rechts*

On Arrival

How do I get to... from here? *Hoe kom ik van hier naar...?*
Is there a bus to...? *Is/Gaat/Rijdt er een bus naar...?*
railway station *station*
I want a ticket to... *Ik wil graag een kaartje naar...*
single (one way) *enkele reis*
return (round-trip) *retour/heen en terug*
first/second class *eerste/tweede klas*
Do you have any vacancies? *Hebt u een kamer vrij?*
a single room *een eenpersoonskamer*
a double room *een tweepersoonskamer*
What is the charge per night? *Hoeveel is het per nacht?*
May I see the room? *Kan ik de kamer bekijken?*

Emergencies

Help/Stop! *Help/Stop!*
Call a doctor/an ambulance *Bel een dokter/een ziekenwagen*
Call the police/fire brigade *Bel de politie/brandweer*
Where is the nearest telephone/hospital? *Waar is de dichtstbijzijnde telefoon/het dichtstbijzijnde ziekenhuis?*
I do not feel well *Ik voel me niet goed/lekker*
I have lost my passport/money/handbag *Ik heb mijn paspoort/geld/handtas verloren*

Shopping

How much is it? *Hoeveel is/kost het?*
Where can I buy...? *Waar kan ik... kopen?*
Have you got...? *Hebt u...?*
Can I have...? *Mag ik... hebben?*
What size is it? *Welke maat is het?*
too much *te veel*
each *per stuk*
cheap/expensive *goedkoop/duur*
I will take it *Ik neem/koop het*
Do you take credit cards? *Aanvaardt u kredietkaarten?*

the bill *de rekening*
I am a vegetarian *Ik ben vegetariër*
What do you recommend *Wat beveelt u aan?*
I'd like... *Ik wil/zou graag...*
I'd like to order *Ik wil bestellen/zou graag bestellen*
That is not what I ordered *Dit is niet wat ik besteld heb*
Is smoking permitted? *Is roken toegestaan?/Mag er gerookt worden?*

Days of the Week

Sunday *Zondag*
Monday *Maandag*
Tuesday *Dinsdag*
Wednesday *Woensdag*
Thursday *Donderdag*
Friday *Vrijdag*
Saturday *Zaterdag*

Numbers

0 *nul*
1 *een*
2 *twee*
3 *drie*
4 *vier*
5 *vijf*
6 *zes*
7 *zeven*
8 *acht*
9 *negen*
10 *tien*
11 *el*
12 *twaalf*
13 *dertien*
14 *veertien*
15 *vijftien*
16 *zestien*
17 *zeventien*
18 *achttien*
19 *negentien*
20 *twintig*
21 *een en twintig*
30 *dertig*
40 *veertig*
50 *vijftig*
60 *zestig*
70 *zeventig*
80 *tachtig*
90 *negentig*
100 *honderd*
200 *tweehonderd*
1,000 *duizend*

As a rule, the 'hard consonants' such as t, k, s and p are pronounced almost the same as in English, but sometimes softer. Other pronunciations differ as follows: *j = y; v = f; je = yer; tje = ch; ee = ay; oo = o; ij = eay; a = u.*

Is there a bank near here? *Is er hier een bank in de buurt?*
I want to change some pounds/dollars *Ik zou graag ponden/dollars wisselen*
chemist *de apotheek*
department store *het warenhuis*
market *de markt*
supermarket *de supermarkt*
receipt *de kassabon*
postcard *de briefkaart*
stamp *de postzegel*

Sightseeing

I am looking for... *Ik zoek...naar*
Where is...? *Waar is hier...?*
tourist information office *de toeristische dienst*
museum *het museum*
church *de kerk*
exhibition *de tentoonstelling*
When does the museum open/close? *Wanneer is het museum open/gesloten?*
free *gratis*

Dining Out

breakfast *het ontbijt*
lunch *de lunch/het middageten*
dinner *het diner/avondeten*
meal *de maaltijd*
menu *de (spijs) kaart/het menu*
Can we see the menu? *Kunnen we de (spijs) kaart bekijken?*
first course *het voorgerecht*
main course *het hoofdgerecht*

Below: tourist areas will have menus in English.

Literature and Theatre

The city of Bruges has long provided a rich backdrop for literary works of religious inspiration, political intrigue and romance. This section introduces writers and dramatists for whom Bruges has provided creative stimulation, as well as a selection of contemporary Flemish writers who have made their mark on the Dutch-language scene. Pageant and performance also have a long tradition in Bruges and are continued today in annual festivals, while the scattering of theatres put on an excellent programme of contemporary fare.

Writers and Dramatists

Bruges had its first literary boom in medieval times. The then Cathedral of St Donatian's on the Burg had a great library, a music school and a scriptorium, where illuminated manuscripts were produced. Bookshops were clustered around the cathedral and attracted pioneers of the trade: William Caxton produced the first printed book in the English language in Bruges in 1474, a *Recuyell of the Histories of Troy*, ordered by Margaret of York, Duchess of Burgundy, before he left to introduce printing in England.

Pre-20th Century

To learn more about the Bruges-inspired revolt against the French in 1302, read **Hendrik Conscience**'s novel *De Leeuw van Vlaanderen* (The Lion of Flanders, 1838). In nearby Damme, the poet **Jacob van Maerlant** (1235–1300) was the greatest Flemish poet of the Middle Ages, and remained the most popular for centuries after his death. He wrote long didactic poems. **Charles de Coster**'s

Above: an illustration of poet Jacob van Maerlant.

The Glorious Adventures of Tijl Uilenspiegel (1867, *see p.17*), inspired by a medieval character, gave the same village its legendary hero.

The Catholic priest and teacher **Guido Gezelle** (1830–

99) was a one-man literary movement, who gave Flemish poetry a new lease of life with his volume *Kerkhofblommen* (Graveyard Flowers, 1858), a mixture of literary Dutch and the dialect of West Flanders.

Left: Hugo Claus (centre), pictured in Paris in 1955.

which are now in their third TV series. All based in Bruges, his stories centre on murder investigations carried out by two police officers.

Hugo Claus (1929–2008) was the most important Flemish writer of the post-World War II period. He received more awards than any other Dutch-language writer, and his work has been translated into 20 languages. His *Het verdriet van België* (1983; The Sorrow of Belgium) – an epic story of collaboration during the Nazi era – is essential reading for anyone who wants to understand modern Belgium. Claus was born in Bruges.

Bart Moeyaert (b.1964) was born and grew up in Bruges, but now lives in Antwerp. A prize-winning author, he has also had several books translated into English, including novels for young adults which deal with family problems, and *Brothers*, a collection of stories that describe his life growing up as the youngest of seven brothers (www.bartmoeyaert.com).

Peter Verhelst (b.1962), another Bruges-born writer who moved away, this time to Ghent, writes poems, novels and poetic texts for dance and theatre productions. His poem for Brugge 2002, the city's year as European Capital of Culture, is engraved into the seat-backs of the Concertgebouw.

Paul De Wispelaere (b.1928), also born in Bruges, is a literary critic and novelist, essayist and lecturer in Dutch-language literature. Editor for years of literary journals, his works are avant-garde and examine the quest for identity and the relationship between literature and life.

Texas-born calligrapher Brody Neuenschwander – who worked with Peter Greenaway on the films *Prospero's Books* (1991) and *The Pillow Book* (1996) – lives in Bruges. His work frequently features in exhibitions and performance pieces.

His ideas and beliefs brought him into conflict with the church and educational authorities, and he abandoned poetry in the 1870s in favour of writing essays and doing translations. Gezelle returned to his first love in *Tijdkrans* (Time's Garland, 1893) and *Rijmsnoer* (String of Rhymes, 1897), poems dealing with nature, religion and Flemish nationalism that show an original use of rhyme, metaphor and sound.

Georges Rodenbach (1855–98) never lived in Bruges but immortalised the city in his 1892 novel *Bruges-la-Morte*. It tells the story of a widower who has retreated to Bruges to grieve for his young wife in a city chosen for its silence, monotony and melancholy. The novel provoked a

'cult of Bruges' among Symbolist artists and poets – Mallarmé, Rodin and Proust were fans – and inspired Thomas Mann (*Death in Venice*), Korngold's opera *Die tote Stadt* (1920) and, it has been claimed, Hitchcock's *Vertigo*.

20th Century and Beyond

Pieter Aspe (b.1953) writes crime fiction best-sellers

Below: the novelist Georges Rodenbach.

Above: the elegant Stadsschouwburg theatre.

Founded in 1888, this shop sells literature in several languages, as well as international newspapers and magazines. The travel bookshop next door (Mon–Sat 9.30am–12.30pm, 1.30–6pm) sells international guide books and maps.

Bookshops

Boekhandel Raaklijn
Sint-Jakobsstraat 7; tel: 050 33 67 20; www.boekhandel raaklijn.be; Mon–Sat 9am–6pm; bus: 0/Centrum; map.134 B4
Delightful bookshop just off the Markt, a local favourite, which stocks a wide selection of fiction and non-fiction in Dutch, French and English.

Brugse Boekhandel
Dijver 2; tel: 050 33 29 52; www.brugseboekhandel.be; Mon 9.30am–noon, 1.30–6.30pm, Tue–Sat 8.30am–noon, 1.30–6.30pm; bus: 0/Centrum; map p.134 C3

Canalside bookshop selling a broad range of books, newspapers and maps, including many in English.

FNAC
Markt 18–19; tel: 050 47 62 62; www.fnac.be; Mon–Sat 10am–6.30pm, Fri until 7pm; bus: 0/Centrum; map.132 C4
This French chainstore is an emporium of music, books, DVDs, games and multimedia, plus audiovisual goods.

De Reyghere
Markt 12–13; tel: 050 33 34 03; www.dereyghere.be; Mon–Sat 8.30am–6.15pm; bus: 0/Centrum; map p.134 C4

Theatre

Cultuurcentrum Brugge/ Stadsschouwburg
Vlamingstraat 29 (Stadsschouwburg); tel: 050 44 30 40; www.cultuurcentrumbrugge.be; bus: 0/Centrum; map p.132 C1
The Bruges cultural centre is a centralised arts organisation for seven performance venues in the city centre and the nearby suburbs. The most prominent venue is the Stadsschouwburg, the elegant city theatre, on Vlamingstraat 29, while the programme encompasses everything from classical and contemporary drama to music and dance.

English Theatre of Bruges
Walplein 23; tel: 050 68 79 45; www.tematema.com; bus: 1; map p.134 C2
Recently relocated, this small English-language theatre hosts professional English-language productions. Its staple

Below: the well-stocked De Reyghere bookshop.

Above: a scene from cult film *Malpertuis*.

she seeks her true path in life. Fred Zinnemann's picture was based on a fictionalised account of a Belgian nun's true story, and was shot on location in Bruges.

Malpertuis (1971). Cultish horror film directed by Belgian Harry Kümel. Orson Welles stars as a dying patriarch who leaves his mansion to a group of heirs on the condition that they must live there for the rest of their lives. Behind its closed doors are a nightmarish assortment of creatures and characters from mythology.

In Bruges (2008). Colin Farrell and Brendan Gleeson star in this comedy-drama as hit men lying low in Bruges after a job gone wrong. To tourism bosses' delight, Martin McDonagh's slick-talking film lent the city a darker vibe, reaching a market that may once have been put off by its traditional, twee reputation.

show is *Bruges Abridged!*, a half-hour one-man comedy tour of Bruges, showing five times daily except Mondays.

De Werf

Werfstraat 108; tel: 050 33 05 29; www.dewerf.be; bus: 13; map p.132 B3

Contemporary drama plays at this popular jazz club.
SEE ALSO MUSIC AND DANCE, P.93

Film in Bruges

The Nun's Story (1959). Audrey Hepburn portrays a young woman in turmoil as

A vast medieval pageant takes place in Bruges every five years in August. The **Praalstoet van de Gouden Boom** (Pageant of the Golden Tree) was conceived in 1958 and recalls the sumptuous marriage in Damme of the Duke of Burgundy, Charles the Bold, to English Princess Margaret of York, in 1468. A great procession and tournament (the 'Tournament of the Golden Tree') was held in the Markt to celebrate the occasion, and it is this that the pageant celebrates, with 2,000 participants. The last two events have made an attempt to incorporate the history of Flanders into the festivities, and the struggle of the lower and merchant classes against their rulers (who were of course French-speaking). The next pageant takes place in 2012.

Below: *In Bruges* has given the city an edgier reputation.

Monuments

One monument stands head and shoulders above the competition: the Belfort (Belfry) on the Markt square, one of Bruges' most popular attractions, whose clocktower and carillon make it a handy landmark when you are finding your way around. This chapter also highlights smaller – and quieter – places that, besides the city's churches and museums *(see pages 46–51 and 82–91)*, help tell the story of Bruges, from a string of windmills and fortified gates around the former city walls, to elite archery and crossbow clubs founded at the time of the crusades.

Belfort

Markt 7; tel: 050 44 81 11; www.brugge.be/musea; daily 9.30am–5pm; entrance charge; bus: 0/Centrum; map p.134 C4

Dominating the Markt, the skyline, and the earshot of anyone nearby, the Belfort (Belfry) dates from the 13th century. The final storey (with the clock) was built in the 15th century. A wooden spire once crowned the tower, but was destroyed, first by lightning in 1493, and then by fire in 1741, leaving it with its current truncated look. Look closely and you may observe that the 83m (272ft) tower leans very slightly to the south-east, by 1.2m (4ft) at its summit.

The climb to the top is 366 steps, and rewards with a 360-degree view (the best time to visit is early morning or late afternoon). The second-floor treasury is where the town seal and charters used to be locked behind the intricate Romanesque grilles (built 1292), each requiring nine separate keys to open them: the burgomaster (mayor) and the eight trade guilds' leaders held one key each, so the doors could only be opened with the agreement of them all.

Further up is the 6-tonne great bell, and at the top the 47-piece carillon, which plays a different peal every quarter-hour. The bells are controlled either manually by the city bell-ringer, who sits in a room just below and gives regular concerts; or, more commonly, by a rotating metal drum.

Twenty-six of the 47 bells in the Belfort carillon are originals, cast by Joris Dumery in the 18th century. His bell-foundry is honoured in Boeveriestraat, near where it was sited, with a large bell that used to hang in the Belfort: the *Dumeryklok*

City walls were thrown up around the inner canal circuit in the aftermath of Charles the Good's assassination in 1127. A second line of walls, punctuated by nine city gates, whose outline is preserved in the ring canal and its park, was built during the 14th century. These were dismantled between 1782–4 by order of the Austrian emperor.

Below: the Belfort towers over Bruges' centre.

Gentpoort

Gentpoortstraat; tel: 050 44 81 11; www.brugge.be/musea; open to public by arrangement only; entrance charge (free for children under 13 years old); bus: 1, 11; map p.135 D2

One of four remaining

Monuments

Left: a coat-of-arms on the Oud Tolhuis.

> The coat of arms on the facade (1477) of the Oud Tolhuis belongs to the Dukes of Luxembourg. Pierre of Luxembourg, Knight of the Golden Fleece, had the concession to levy import taxes on goods entering the ports of Bruges.

(Market Halls) and courtyard (13th–15th century), built to replace an earlier wooden structure on the same site, and with later additions made due to fire. For three centuries this was the pride of the city, and the focal point of its commercial life. It would have been crammed with traders, the air heavy with the scent of spices brought by Venetian merchants. City statutes and proclamations were announced from the balcony over the market entrance. It has recently come back into use as a commercial and exhibition centre. In front of the Hallen is a bronze replica of the Belfort and Hallen, with Braille inscriptions.

medieval city gates, recently renovated. The other three are Kruispoort (Holy Cross Gate), Smedenpoort and Ezelpoort (Donkey Gate) in the north-west. Note the different architectural styles of the gates when viewed from outside the city limits (fierce and fortified) or within (elegant and turreted).

Groot Seminarie – Ter Duinen Abdij

Potterierei 72; tel: 050 33 03 62; www.grootseminariebrugge.be; open to public by arrangement only; bus: 4; map p.133 D3

The Duinen Abdij (Abbey of the Dunes) moved here in the 17th century from Koksijde on the coast – hence its name. Since 1833 it has been the Episcopal Seminary, and occasionally hosts exhibitions. You can visit its 18th-century church, gardens, greenhouse – and large meadow – with permission, obtainable (perhaps) at the main entrance.

Hallen

Markt 7; free; bus: 0/Centrum; map p.134 C4
Below the Belfort are the heftily-proportioned Hallen

Oud Tolhuis

Jan van Eyckplein 2; not open to public; bus: 4, 14; map p.132 C1

Below: the Gentpoort guards the eastern entrance to the city.

79

Above: the Poertoren.

Behind the pointed gable of the Gothic Oud Tolhuis (Old Customs House) is a 13th-century merchant's house, with spacious rooms on lower floors for storing goods and living quarters upstairs. Boats entering the city had to visit this house to pay taxes on goods brought in from the outer ports of Damme and Sluis. The adjoining sliver of a house (15th century) was occupied by *pijnders* (porters), who are represented in stone carvings at the base of a pillar. Next door used to be the public weighing house. The combined buildings are now the seat of the provincial library, which holds 600 religious manuscripts and early printed books.

Poertoren

Begijnenvest; not open to public; bus: 1; map p.134 B1
The Poertoren (Powder Tower) at the southern end of the Minnewater lake was built in 1398 and is the only one of the city walls' defensive towers to have survived. It is named after the gunpowder and munitions that it stored.

Poortersloge

Academiestraat 14; not open to public; bus: 4, 14; map p.132 C1
Overlooking Jan van Eyck-plein, the tower of the Poortersloge (Burghers' Lodge) was the meeting place for the wealthiest bankers and merchants of Bruges. It dates from the 14th century; on its facade there is a statue of the bear that features in the city's coat of arms. It was also the emblem of a jousting club that held events in the marketplace outside. Used as the city's fine arts academy until 1890, it now houses the city archives.

Provinciaal Hof

Markt 2; not open to the public; bus: 0/Centrum; map p.134 C4
On the east side of the Markt stands the Provinciaal Hof (Provincial House), built 1887–92 as the seat for the West Flanders provincial government and governor, who represents the royal court and federal government in the province.

Schuttersgilde Sint-Joris

Stijn Streuvelsstraat 59; tel: 050 44 87 11; open by arrangement only; entrance charge; bus: 6, 16; map p.133 E1
Unlike at St Sebastian's, the boys of the Schuttersgilde Sint-Joris (St George's Archers' Guild) were crossbowmen. Their ornate guild-house contains a collection of crossbows, as well as the guild's archives. The park-sized garden has a vertical target-mast and sheltered walkways to protect against falling arrows.

Schuttersgilde Sint-Sebastiaan

Carmersstraat 174; tel: 050 33 16 26; www.sebastiaan sgilde.be; May–Sept Tue–Thur 10am–noon, Sat 2–5pm, Oct–Apr Tue–Thur and Sat 2–5pm; entrance charge; bus: 6, 16; map p133 E2
The Schuttersgilde Sint-Sebastiaan (St Sebastian's Archers' Guild) is an ancient and prestigious longbow club, whose reputation grew from the time of the crusades. Inside is a fine collection of arms, furnishings, gold and silver plate, and other works of art.

Sint-Janshuismolen and Other Windmills

Kruisvest; tel: 050 44 81 11; www.brugge.be/musea; May–Aug Tue–Sat 9.30am–12.30pm, 1.30–5pm; entrance charge; bus: 6, 16; map p.133 E2
Dotted around the north-east perimeter of the city are four windmills, the only remaining examples from the 29 that stood along the city walls during the 19th century. Two are open to the public and still mill grain. The first, starting from the south, **Bonne Chièremolen**, is no longer in use. Standing on wooden stilt supports, it was built in 1888

Below: the Bonne Chieremolen windmill.

Above: the Stadhuis is situated on the Burg.

at Olsene in East Flanders, and moved to its present location in 1911.

Sint-Janshuismolen (St John's House Mill) is operated throughout the summer as a museum piece, with a miller to show visitors around. This venerable structure, accessed via a vertiginous staircase, earned a living by twirling its blades here from 1770 to 1914. It was restored in 1964.

Next is **Nieuwe Papegaaimolen**, which was used as an oil-mill at Beveren-IJzer in West Flanders and rebuilt here in 1970. It is no longer in use.

The final mill of the quartet is the **Koeleweimolen** (Cool Meadow Mill; Kruisvest; July–Aug Tue–Sat 9.30am–12.30pm, 1.30–5pm; entrance charge), dating from 1765 and employed at Meulebeke in West Flanders until it was rebuilt here in 1996.

Stadhuis

Burg 12; tel: 050 44 87 11; www.brugge.be/musea; Tue–Sun 9.30am–5pm; entrance charge; bus: 0/Centrum; map p.135 C4

The town hall's magnificent first-floor is the only part of the building open to visitors. Its majestic Gothic Hall incorporates a rib-vaulted ceiling and polychrome decoration, renovated in the late 19th century. The ceiling is decorated with keystones depicting biblical scenes and its vaults rest on original stone consoles portraying the months of the year in scenes of rural life, and the four elements, a common Renaissance theme.

In the adjoining Maritime Chamber, an exhibition tells the story of the city's government through historic manuscripts, maps, engravings and paintings. Take time to study Marcus Gerards' 1562 engraving of the city and imagine how he must have climbed all the city's towers to get such a unique bird's eye view.

SEE ALSO ARCHITECTURE, P.27

Below: the grand interior of the Stadhuis.

Illustrious past members of St Sebastian's Archers' Guild include England's King Charles II, who paid for the banqueting hall, and his brother Henry, who were both in Bruges in exile from Oliver Cromwell. Charles formed a royal regiment of guards here in 1656, which accompanied him back to London when the monarchy was restored in 1660. All British monarchs since have been honorary members of the guild.

Museums and Galleries

Even if you have wall-to-wall sunshine during your trip to Bruges, make time to step inside at least one of the city's museums. None require even a half-day's attention, yet each provides a fascinating insight into some aspect of the town's chequered history. Take your pick from priceless paintings commissioned by the wealthiest individuals in medieval Europe, glittering church artefacts, early medical instruments, implements of torture or the everyday household set-up of the poor, who eked out a living making lace.

Markt and Burg

Heilig Bloedbasiliek museum

Burg 10; tel: 050 33 67 92; www.holyblood.com; Apr–Sept daily 9.30am–noon, 2–6pm, Oct–Mar Thur–Tue 10am–noon, 2–4pm, Wed 10am–noon; entrance charge; bus: 0/Centrum; map p.134 C4

On the right just before you enter the upper chapel, the one-room basilica museum contains items relating to the relic of holy blood and the basilica: precious and elaborate reliquaries, a Pieter Pourbus painting (1556) showing the 31 members of the Noble Brotherhood of the Holy Blood, and a curious 15th-century manuscript showing the robes worn by the brotherhood, which still provides inspiration to participants in the annual procession *(see p.46)*. A tiny gold crown with precious stones belonging to Mary of Burgundy looks surprisingly crude in manufacture; and there is a ripped-open lead box that concealed the relic, first, for six years from 1578, when Bruges became a Protestant

city and the basilica a public library, and again during the French Revolution (1797).
SEE ALSO ARCHITECTURE, P.24; CHURCHES, P.46

Bruggemuseum-Brugse Vrije

Burg 11a, tel: 050 44 87 11; www.brugge.be/musea; daily 9.30am–12.30pm, 1.30–5pm; entrance charge; bus: 0/Centrum; map p.135 C4

The Paleis van het Brugse Vrije (Liberty of Bruges Palace) has one room that can be visited: the Renaissance Hall, containing a great black marble and oak chimneypiece, created 1528–31 by painter Lanceloot Blondeel, in tribute to Charles V, Holy Roman Emperor.

The Liberty of Bruges was a geographical concept, referring to the district around the city. The four burgomasters and 28 aldermen of the Liberty met in this room, which has been restored to its original condition, complete with aldermen's benches and big brass inkwells. Pride of place goes to the wall containing the black Dinant marble fireplace with an alabaster frieze and

carved oak chimneypiece. This is one of the most memorable artworks in Bruges: the carving is on a monumental scale, covering an entire wall.

The fireplace celebrates the imperial army's victory at Pavia over Francis I of France in 1525. The Treaty of Madrid, which was signed the following year, broke Belgium free from French domination. Charles, with raised sceptre and the orb of empire in his hands, stands in the centre beneath the double-headed eagle emblem of the Habsburg Empire. He is flanked by his grandparents: Emperor Maximilian of Austria, Duchess Mary of Burgundy, King Ferdinand II of

> The Bruggemuseum-Brugse Vrije is situated inside the Landhuis van het Brugse Vrije (Liberty of Bruges Palace), an early 18th-century neo-Classical building on the site of an older structure that formerly housed the law courts – a 16th-century facade can be seen from the canalside of the building.

Left: Jan v an Eyck's *Madonna and Child with Canon Joris van der Paele* can be seen at the Groeningemuseum.

bus: 1; map p.134 C3
The city's archaeological museum contains a small but interesting collection of pottery, glass, leather, wood, stone figurines and tomb paintings, including vestiges of the former St Donatian's Cathedral. The collection is presented in a lively, educational way, drawing parallels and contrasts between daily life in the Stone Age, the Middle Ages and the present.

Arentshuis
Dijver 16; tel: 050 44 87 11; www.brugge.be/musea; Tue–Sun 9.30am–5pm; entrance charge; bus: 0/Centrum; map p.134 C3
This Arents House is divided between the ground floor, used for temporary exhibitions of the Groeningemuseum, and upstairs, which is devoted to the extensive collection of Welsh artist Frank Brangwyn (1867–1956). A disciple of the Arts and Crafts

Aragon and Queen Isabella I of Castile.

The alabaster friezes depict the biblical tale of Susanna and the Elders, by whom she is falsely accused and who get stoned to death. The craftsmanship of the ensemble is quite overwhelming, but the brass handholds for the rural noblemen to use

while drying their boots are the sort of domestic touch that everyone remembers.

South

Bruggemuseum-Archeologie
Mariastraat 36a; tel: 050 44 87 11; www.brugge.be/musea; Tue–Sun 9.30am–12.30pm, 1.30–5pm; entrance charge;

Below: a selection of pottery in the Archeologisch Museum.

Above: *L'attentat* by René Magritte, from the Surrealist collection at the Groeningemuseum.

Movement and apprentice to its greatest exponent, William Morris, Brangwyn was born in Bruges and returned to paint here, donating most of his work to the city in 1936. His realistic paintings depict industrial life in the docks and factories, and there are items of furniture, prints and rugs which he designed.

The modern sculpture in the garden is Rik Poot's *Four Horsemen of the Apocalypse*, representing the horrors of war, death, famine and revolution.

Begijnhuisje museum

Begijnhof 30; tel: 050 33 00 11; Mon–Sat 9.30am–noon, 1.45–5pm, Sun 10.45am–noon, 1.45–5pm; entrance charge; bus: 1; map p.134 B2

This small house (*huisje*) in the corner of the Begijnhof's courtyard gives a glimpse into the life of a *begijn* – a religious woman similar to a nun but who took no vows, lived alone and supported herself by private means or by teaching, caring for the sick or making lace. Staffed by Benedictine nuns who now occupy the Begijnhof, and in a white-washed cottage, it resembles a typical Beguine's house, still, essentially, in its 17th-century condition, with red-tiled floor, traditional furniture and a small cloister garden with a well.

SEE ALSO BEGUINAGES, P.29

Diamantmuseum

Katelijnestraat 43; tel: 050 34 20 56; www.diamondhouse.net; Tue–Sun 10.30am–5.30pm;

Below: detail from Rik Poot's *Four Horsemen of the Apocalypse.*

Below: an ornamental fountain outside the Groeningemuseum.

entrance charge; bus 1; map p.134 C2

This museum documents the history of diamond polishing – a technique thought to have been invented by Bruges goldsmith Lodewijk van Berquem in the mid-15th century. On display you will find a reconstruction of van Berquem's workshop, examples of tools and machinery used in diamond polishing, plus models, paintings and rare rock samples. Daily demonstrations (at 12.15pm) further illustrate the technique.

Groeningemuseum

Dijver 12; tel: 050 44 87 11; www.brugge.be/musea; Tue–Sun 9.30am–5pm; entrance charge; bus: 0/Centrum; map p.134 C3

A pathway leads from the Dijver to the Municipal Fine Arts Museum (Stedelijk Museum voor Schone Kunsten), more commonly known as the Groeningemuseum. The gallery is relatively small, yet in terms of quality, it deserves to be ranked among the world's great museums. Visitors who are limited for time could restrict their visit to the first four rooms, which are arranged chronologically. The informative audio guide is included in the ticket price.

The collection spans the artistic development of the Low Countries over six centuries and includes works by the so-called 'Flemish Primitives' of the 15th century. Far from being primitive, these painters were responsible for a revolutionary step forward in art, moving away from rigidly religious medieval themes towards portraying real people.

Their realism can be observed in such masterpieces as Jan van Eyck's *Madonna and Child with Canon Joris van der Paele, St*

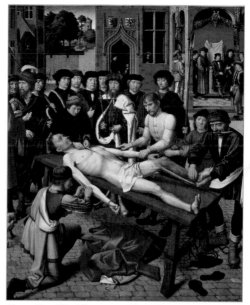

Above: Gerard David's gruesome *The Flaying of Sisamnes* from his two-panel *Judgement of Cambyses* at the Groeningemuseum.

Donatian and St John, and the same artist's *Portrait of Margareta van Eyck* (his wife); Hans Memling's *Moreel Triptych*; Hugo van der Goes' *Death of the Virgin*; the fascinating *Martyrdom of St Hippolytus* (c.1468), a triptych by Dirk Bouts with a side panel by Hugo van der Goes, and works by Rogier van der Weyden, Pieter Pourbus and Gerard David.

Artist Jan Van Eyck, whose works can be seen in the Groeningemuseum, is said to have perfected – although not invented – the technique of oil painting: he mixed powder colours, egg white, water and resin in a new paint formula that allowed for greater variety of colour and thinner application; the recipe was a fiercely guarded secret among Netherlandish artists.

A nonchalantly gruesome work is the *Judgement of Cambyses* (1498) by Gerard David, showing a corrupt Persian judge being flayed alive by torturers. Another wonderful painting is *The Last Judgement* by Hieronymous Bosch, a grim but complicated account of the trials that await sinners in the afterlife. Do not ignore less advertised paintings such as *The Town Docks at Bruges* (1653) by Hendrik van Minderhout, which gives an idea of the size of the merchant ships that routinely called at Bruges. In later rooms, there are works by Belgian Symbolists including Fernand Khnopff, Flemish Expressionists Constant Permeke, Gustave De Smet, Jan Brusselmans and Gustave van de Woestyne, and Surrealists René Magritte and Paul Delvaux.

A fantastic Burgundian Gothic tracery of rose-coloured stone with high towers and arched windows (much of it 19th-century reconstruction), the Palace of the Lords of Gruuthuse was a refuge for the exiled English kings Edward IV in 1470–71 and Charles II in 1656.

Bruggemuseum-Gruuthuse

Dijver 17; tel: 050 44 87 11; www.brugge.be/musea; Tue–Sun 9.30am–5pm; entrance charge; bus: 0/Centrum, 1; map p.134 C3

This former palace, which belonged to the Lords of Gruuthuse, is part of the city's historical museum (Bruggemuseum) network and contains a wealth of decorative arts, recalling life as lived – mainly by the high and mighty – in Bruges from the 13th–19th century. Parts of the museum are closed for renovation until 2011, so not all 2,500 objects in the collection – paintings, sculptures, musical instruments, lace, silk, tapestries, furniture, weapons

Above: exterior of the Gruuthuse Museum.

and glassware – will be on full display for a while. Highlights include the upper-floor oratory, a 1520 bust of the young Charles V and a guillotine (which was used).

Lodewijk van Gruuthuse's oak-panelled Gothic oratory dates from 1472. The private chapel abuts the adjacent Onze-Lieve-Vrouwekerk *(see*

right), and afforded Lodewijk and his family an undisturbed, overhead view of the altar and of the tombs of Duke Charles the Bold of Burgundy and his daughter Duchess Mary. The Gruuthuse family motto, *Plus Est En Vous* (There Is More In You), can be seen above an arch in the ornate reception hall.

One of the oldest rooms is the large kitchen with a vast hearth and a cauldron weighing 680kg.

The guillotine displayed on the ground floor was purchased by the city of Bruges in 1796 and tested on a sheep before being used to carry out death sentences. At the time, the guillotine was considered an enlightened innovation, since it enabled swift and efficient execution.

Onze-Lieve-Vrouwekerk

Mariastraat; tel: 050 44 87 11; www.brugge.be/musea; Mon–Fri 9.30am–5pm, Sat 9.30am–4.45pm, Sun 1.30–5pm; entrance charge; bus: 1; map p.134 C3

The most valuable artwork in the Onthaalkerk Onze-Lieve-

Below: tapestries and other artefacts on display at the Gruuthuse Museum.

Above: the church of Onze-Lieve-Vrouwekerk is rich with important artworks.

Vrouw (Church of Our Lady), Michelangelo's *Madonna and Child* statue, can be viewed by all visitors, but you need to buy a ticket to see the church's other treasures, which are located in the side aisles, ambulatory and choir. Here you can see the magnificent side-by-side tombs of Charles the Bold and his daughter Mary of Burgundy. Charles was killed in 1477 at the Battle of Nancy (after his band of Italian mercenaries defected to the other side), while Mary died in a riding accident in 1482. Her sarcophagus, made from black marble surmounted by a graceful, reclining image of her in bronze, dates from 1502 and is a superb work of late Gothic art. Her father's, also furnished with a recumbent image of the deceased in bronze, was not completed until the mid-16th century. By that time the Renaissance style was in

vogue, and it is interesting to compare the differences between the two today.

Beneath the tombs are vaults with medieval frescoes uncovered in recent digs, while notable paintings include a *Last Supper* and *Adoration of the Shepherds* by Pieter Pourbus, Gerard David's *Transfiguration*, a painting of the Crucifixion by Anthony van Dyck, as well as works by Dirk Bouts and Hugo van der Goes.

SEE ALSO ARCHITECTURE, P.24; CHURCHES, P.47

Memling in Sint-Jan

Mariastraat 38; tel: 050 44 87 11; www.brugge.be/musea; Tue–Sun 9.30am–5pm; entrance charge; bus: 1; map p.134 B3
A small but priceless collection of paintings by German-born painter Hans Memling (c.1440–1494) are displayed in the 15th century chapel of the Sint-Janshospitaal (St John's hospital), the main draw of this museum. Mem-

ling lived in Bruges from 1465 until his death, and four of the six works here were commissioned especially for this chapel. Each work testifies to his captivating attention to detail and mastery of realism. They include the *Mystic Triptych of St John*, part of an altarpiece that has side-panel images of John the Baptist and John the Evangelist; the *Adoration of the Magi*, notable for its serene image

The In&Uit tourist bureau on 't Zand *(see p.55)* sells combined entry tickets to museums that represent significant savings: the Brugge City Card, €35 for 48 hours or €45 for 72 hours, gives access to 23 museums, a boat ride or bus tour plus further discounts on car parks, bike hire, cultural events and shopping – see www.bruggecitycard.be. Alternatively, a three-day ticket valid for entry to five of the municipal museums is €15.

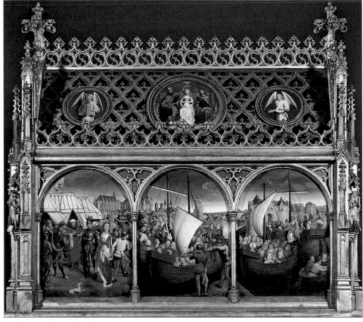

Above: Hans Memling's wooden *Shrine of St Ursula*.

of the Virgin Mary; and the exquisite *Shrine of St Ursula* (*c.*1489), a wooden reliquary in the shape of a Gothic church, on whose panels Memling painted several scenes from the life of St Ursula, including her martyrdom by the Huns at Cologne (along with a reputed 11,000 virgins who had set out with her on a pilgrimage to Rome). One of the greatest art treasures in the country, the shrine was commissioned by two sisters who worked in the church.

The rest of the former hospital, which was founded in the 12th century and is one of the oldest surviving in Europe, contains objects telling the story of medical care in medieval times. In what were once the wards, there is an exhibition of historical documents and rather alarming surgical instruments. The 17th-century pharmacy (closed 11.45am–2pm) has a carved relief showing patients sleeping two to a bed. There is a strong sense of tradition in the place, enhanced by the informative visitor centre.

> Construction of Sint-Janshospitaal (St John's Hospital) began in the 12th century and continued over the centuries; parts of the complex continued to function as a working hospital right up until 1976. You can see the later buildings if you wander around the courtyard at the back of the museum, where the former hospital is now used as a conference centre, shops and cafés.

West

Forum+

't Zand 34; tel: 050 44 87 11; www.brugge.be/musea; Tue–Sun 9.30am–5pm; entrance charge; bus: 0/Centrum; map p.134 B3

A small contemporary art space within the city's Concertgebouw (Concert Hall; *see p.92*) offers the opportunity to get a peek inside this modern landmark and a view from its heights. It hosts three exhibitions a year each showcasing the work of one particular artist.

Sint-Salvatorskathedraal

Zuidzandstraat; tel: 050 33 68 41; www.sintsalvator.be; Sun–Fri 2–5pm; entrance charge; bus: 0/Centrum; map p.134 B3

The treasury of Sint-Salvatorskathedraal (St Saviour's Cathedral), in the right transept, is home to paintings by Dirk Bouts, Adriaen Ysenbrandt, Lancelot Blondeel and Pieter Pourbus, and other ecclesiastical riches, including brass tomb plates, reliquaries and vestments,

and a piece of a tunic which allegedly belonged to St Bridget of Ireland (d.523).
SEE ALSO CHURCHES, P.49

North
Choco-Story
Wijnzakstraat 2; tel: 050 61 22 37; www.choco-story.be; daily 10am–5pm except two weeks mid-Jan; entrance charge; bus: 0/Centrum, 6, 16; map p.132 C1
No visit to Bruges is complete without sampling a praline – or three – of finest Belgian chocolate. This museum caters to visitors in need of a bit of culture to accompany their daily fix of something chocolatey because it details the history of chocolate but without overlooking the importance of tasting. A privately-owned museum (owned by a Belgian food industry magnate who also owns the Fries Museum, below), it occupies a historic building on the corner of Sint-Jansplein.
SEE ALSO CHILDREN, P.43

Above: statue at the Potterie-museum.

Friet Museum
Vlamingstraat 33; tel: 050 34 01 50; www.frietmuseum.be; daily 10am–5pm except two weeks mid-Jan; entrance charge; bus: 0/Centrum, 3, 13; map p.132 C1
The Fries Museum occupies the historic Genuese Loge merchants house, and is devoted to the history of potatoes and chips, told through artefacts and lengthy wall texts (so not ideal for young children who cannot read). An important part of the history entails restoring to Belgium ownership of a food known worldwide as 'French fries', allegedly the result of confusion on the part of American soldiers after World War I. Little of the historic interior survives, except for the vaulted cellar, which is now the museum café and serves tasty *Belgian* fries.

East
Kantcentrum
Peperstraat 3a; tel: 050 33 00 72; www.kantcentrum.com; Mon–Sat 10am–5pm; entrance charge; bus: 6, 16; map p.133 D1
You may by this stage of your wanders in Bruges have seen enough lace shops and people making lace to last a lifetime. But the Kantcentrum (Lace Centre) is appeal-

Below: *Martyrdom of Saint Hippolytus* by Dieric Bouts the Elder, at Sint-Salvatorskathedraal.

ing, as it is the place where the various strands come together. Next door to the Jeruzalemkerk *(see p.50)* and included on the same entrance ticket, the centre occupies the old Adornes family mansion (the Gothic facade is the only original feature that survives) and the former Jerusalem almshouses founded by the family in the 15th century. The centre is a non-profit-making foundation that aims to continue the work of the Sisters Apostle, who started teaching lace-making in Bruges in 1717. Each after-noon, demonstrations of the craft of bobbin lace are held. The six tiny almshouses make up the museum. The display is rather tired, but there are notable examples of lacework varieties, includ-ing antique specimens. Round the corner in Bal-straat is a shop where you can buy all of the materials you need to have a go at the painstaking art yourself.

SEE ALSO SHOPPING, P.125

Bruggemuseum-Gezelle
Rolweg 64; tel: 050 44 87 11; www.brugge.be/musea; Tue–

Sun 9.30am–12.30pm, 1.30–5pm; entrance charge; bus: 6, 16; map p.133 E2

This museum celebrates the work of Flemish poet-priest Guido Gezelle (1830–99) in the house where he was born. The residence and large walled garden is devoted to the story of his life and work, from his childhood and teach-ing at a seminary to his polit-ical writings and poetry.

Gezelle, whose poetry has been translated into 17 lan-guages, became heavily involved in the Flemish Move-ment: he endeavoured to develop an language distinct from Dutch, including ele-ments of the West Flanders dialect, in which he wrote his poems. A brief hour spent in the house and garden here can be surprisingly rewarding and relaxing, even if you do not know Gezelle's poetry or read Dutch (there is a hand-out in English).

SEE ALSO LITERATURE AND THEATRE, P.74

Bruggemuseum-Volkskunde
Balstraat 43; tel: 050 44 87 11; www.brugge.be/musea; Tue–Sun 9.30am–5pm; entrance charge; bus: 6, 16; map p.133 D1

Below: traditional bobbins, used for the manufacture of lace, at the Kantcentrum.

At its height, in 1840, lace-making in Bruges employed 10,000 women and girls out of a total population of 45,000. Although the Industrial Revolution was well under way by this time, this was still a cottage industry.

Just up the road from the Jeruzalemkerk and Kantcentrum (Lace Centre, *see opposite*), in a row of whitewashed cottages of the former Shoemakers' Guild almshouse, is the Volkskunde (folklore) museum. Modest yet appealing, it offers a peek into what people did in Bruges before they all started working in tourism. The rooms show reconstructed interiors of times past: a primary school class led by a young priest, a living room and clogmaker's, milliner's and cooper's workshops, a pipe room, a pharmacist's and a confectioner's (sweet-making demonstrations are held on Thursday afternoons). In summer, children and adults can play traditional games in the museum garden; and the visit ends in the museum's historic ale house, De Zwarte Kat (The Black Cat).
SEE ALSO CHILDREN, P.44

Lumina Domestica
Wijnzakstraat 2; tel: 050 61 22 37; www.luminadomestica.be; daily 10am–5pm; entrance charge; bus: 6, 16; map p.132 C1

Left: artefacts from the life of poet Guido Gezelle, on display at the Guido Gezellemuseum.

Adjoining the Choco-Story museum *(see p.89)*, this establishment tells the story of domestic lighting, starting with the torch and the oil lamp and tracing 400,000 years of history to the LED. More than 6,000 lamps, collected by an enthusiast, are on display.

Potterie-museum
Potterierei 79; tel: 050 44 87 11; www.brugge.be/musea; Tue–Sun 9.30am–12.30, 1.30–5pm; entrance charge; bus: 4; map p.133 D3
A former hospice founded in 1276, the Potterie-museum adjoins Onze-Lieve-Vrouwter-Potterie (Our Lady of the Pottery) church and contains curious articles related to

The curious assembly of artefacts in the Folklore Museum includes the extensive pipe collection of Belgium's first prime minister, Achille van Acker, who was born in Bruges.

medical care, including a rare collection of lepers' rattles (16th century), and a wealth of furniture dating from the 15th–17th centuries. There are a number of devotional panels, tapestries and medieval sculptures, a triptych by Flemish Primitive Pieter Pourbus and a display of Delftware. Proceed to the church's treasury and feast your eyes on the glittering silverware, several 15th–16th-century Books of Hours and a rare 16th-century Book of Miracles.
SEE ALSO CHURCHES, P.51

Below: iconic poster advertising the Stedelijk Museum voor Volkskunde's traditional ale house, the Black Cat.

Music and Dance

The musical reputation of Bruges has taken off since the new concert hall opened in 2002. True to tradition, it is best known for programming early and sacred music; the vast Festival of Flanders classical music bonanza starts in Bruges each summer. There is also a flourishing network of cultural venues coordinated from the Stadsschouwburg, the municipal theatre, which programmes world music, rock and contemporary dance, in addition to theatre. The Flemish dance scene has an international reputation, bolstered by energetic and cutting-edge troupes who attract companies from around the world to Bruges.

Classical Music

Bruges does not have a great music tradition, but, just as in the visual arts, was a hotbed of creativity during the 15th century, when St Donatian's cathedral was an important musical centre. The most prominent of Bruges composers is possibly **Jacob Obrecht** (1457/8–1505), who wrote at least 30 Mass cycles in the late 15th century. **Gilles Joye** (c.1424–83), in contrast, is known mainly for his secular songs, while **Adrien Basin** (c.1457–98) was one of Charles the Bold's personal singers at the Burgundian court. **Lupus Hellinck** (c.1494–1541) was choirmaster at Onze-Lieve-Vrouwekerk 1521–3, and then at St Donatian's from 1523 until his death, during which time he wrote Masses, motets, German chorales, French chansons, and songs in Flemish. **Clemens non Papa** was priest and choirmaster at St Donatian's from 1544. Known for his polyphonic settings of psalms, he also composed secular motets for Charles V.

The early music tradition of Bruges is celebrated each year in the vast **Festival van Vlaanderen**, a classical music festival that moves across Flanders, starting in Bruges with the pre-Renaissance period, then moving to other Flemish towns, where other traditions are emphasised. *See* www.festival.be.

One of Belgium's leading orchestras, the 60-piece freelance **Symfonieorkest Vlaanderen** (Flanders Symphony Orchestra), is based in Bruges but not in a performance venue, although it performs frequently at the Concertgebouw, *see right*, as well as in other Flemish cities. See www.symfonieorkest.be.

Main Venues

Cactus Musiekcentrum

MaZ, Magdalenastraat 27, 8200 Brugge Sint-Andries; tel: 050 71 68 40; www.cactusmusic.be; bus: 25; map p.138 C3

The main rock, world and alternative concert organiser in Bruges, whose principal venue is the MaZ (Magdalenazaal). It puts on an eclectic concert schedule featuring major international names in rock, pop, country, funk, electronica and experimental, to local young bands. In early July, it holds the three-day Cactus Festival in the Minnewater Park.

Concertgebouw

't Zand 34; tel: 050 47 69 99; box offiice: 070 22 33 02; www.concertgebouw.be; bus: 0/Centrum; map p.134 B3

The terracotta-tiled Concertgebouw (concert hall) is known for the purity of its artistic programming: there is a strong emphasis on classical music performed as the composer would have intended, spanning the whole repertoire up to contemporary classical and electronica. Period instrument ensemble **Anima Eterna**, led by Jos van Immerseel, has been the orchestra in residence since the building opened in 2002.

Carillon concerts take place in the Belfort mid-June–mid-Sept Mon, Wed, Sat 9pm, Sun 2pm, mid-Sept–mid-June Wed 11am, Sat–Sun 2pm. Seating is provided in the Hallen courtyard. See www.carillon-brugge.be.

Left: Bruges has its own annual jazz festival.

Brugge festival, held every two years over one week, focussing on current trends in European jazz (on alternate years, it puts on the smaller Flemish jazz festival). It also hosts contemporary and young people's theatre productions and other types of live music.

Music Shops

FNAC

Markt 18–19; tel: 050 47 62 62; www.fnac.be; Mon–Sat 10am–6.30pm, Fri until 7pm; bus: 0/Centrum; map.132 C4

The Bruges branch of this French music, book and multimedia chainstore opened in 2008. It also sells concert tickets.

Rombaux

Mallebergplaats 13; tel: 050 33 25 75; www.rombaux.be; Mon 2–6.30pm, Tue–Fri 10am–12.30pm, 2–6.30pm, Sat 10am–6pm, plus Sun afternoons towards Christmas; bus: 0/Centrum; map p.135 C4

The sort of place that makes you determine never to shop on the internet again, Rombaux is crammed with everything from classical music to new-wave Flemish folk; staff can track down almost any performer you can name, or sell you a piano, guitar or harp.

Look out for concerts in churches, too. The Sint-Walburgakerk is a regular venue for sacred music concerts during the annual Festival of Flanders, and provides a highly atmospheric setting. Organ recitals are often performed at the intimate Onze-Lieve-Vrouw van Blindekens (Our Lady of the Blind); the Karmelietenkerk hosts concerts of plainsong, among other things.

Touring ballet, dance and opera productions also play at the Concertgebouw, which holds an annual contemporary dance festival in December and co-produces the biennial Jazz Brugge festival with De Werf (see below).
SEE ALSO ARCHITECTURE, P.24

Stadsschouwburg

Vlamingstraat 29; tel: 050 30 01 77; www.cultuurcentrumbrugge.be; bus: 3, 13; map p.132 C1

The neoclassical Stadsschouwburg (city theatre) is now the core of Cultuurcentrum Brugge, a network of cultural venues across the city, which is anything but classical in its programming.

Dance, live music (rock, pop, world and folk) and theatre form the mainstay, but visual art exhibitions also feature. The other venues include a 17th century former chapel, the Hallen complex beneath the Belfort, and the MaZ, used by the Cactus Club.

De Werf

Werfstraat 108; tel: 050 33 05 29; www.dewerf.be; bus: 13; map p.132 B3

This jazz and blues venue has its own record label. It works in close association with renowned Bruges-born jazz pianist and composer Kris Defoort (b.1959), and is the motor behind the **Jazz**

Below: a classical recital at Concertgebouw.

Nightlife

Die-hard clubbers will travel from Bruges to the student centres of Ghent, Antwerp or Kortrijk for a night out, but several bars in the city have dance-floors, and because they are not nightclubs proper, do not charge for entrance, except on special nights. This section details the bars and cafés – mostly quite small places – that come alive after dark; as well as the city's two cinemas, and information for gay visitors to Bruges. Live music and theatre venues are listed elsewhere in this book *(see Music and Dance)*, as are bars and cafés best-suited for chilling out over a beer *(see Cafés and Bars)*.

After Dark

B-In
Zonnekemeers – Oud Sint Jan; tel: 050 31 13 00; www.b-in.be; Tue–Sat 11am–2am; bus: 1; map p.134 B2

Trendy lounge bar in the pedestrianised area behind Memling in Sint-Jan museum, where staff and security drip attitude and customers include Club Brugge football team players, so dress to impress. Live DJ sets every Fri and Sat night.

Café De Vuurmolen
Kraanplein 5; tel: 050 33 00 79; www.vuurmolen.com; daily 10pm–6am; bus: 0/Centrum; map p.132 C1

Fun and up-for-it party-bar, open all day as a regular café with terrace and way after many other places have shut up shop.

De Coulissen
Jacob van Ooststraat 4, Colt Vlamingstraat; Thur–Sun from 9pm; free; bus: 0/Centrum; map p.134 C4

This dimly lit, dance and lounge venue plays R&B, techno and lounge sounds for all ages, but dress up if you want impress the door staff.

Entrance charge on occasional special nights.

Entre Nous
Langestraat 145; tel: 050 34 10 93; www.bauhauszaal.be; parties most Fri and some Sat 10pm–6am; bus: 6, 16; map p.133 E1

New club venue – the first in the city centre – which is part of the ever-expanding Bauhaus youth hostel-hotel-café empire. Check flyers for party details. There are events most weekends, some free, some not.

La Fuente
Vrijdagmarkt 15; tel: 0478 20 33 07; Mon, Tue, Thur, Fri 3pm–3am, Sat 10am–4am, Sun 3pm–4am; bus: 0/Centrum; map p.134 A3

Attractive and friendly bar on the 't Zand square run by a young couple, and popular with a slightly older crowd who just want to let loose to upbeat pop, disco and Latin sounds.

Het Entrepot
Binnenweg 4; tel: 050 61 02 48; www.het-entrepot.be; occasional weekends 9pm–4am; entrance charge; bus: 14

An old customs building just outside the ring canal, north of the city, which hosts anything from dance classes and jam

sessions to organised club nights some weekends, frequented by a youthful crowd. Check website or flyers and posters around town and be sure to have a means of getting back to the city later.

Joey's Café
Zilverpand; tel: 050 34 12 64; Mon–Sat 11.30am–2am, 3am or 4am; bus: 0/Centrum; map p.134 B3

Jazzy sounds play late into the night at this small café (with a large outdoor terrace) in the Zilverpand shopping centre, where no one will complain about the noise. Run by a friendly local musician, this is a relaxed place to enjoy good music long after most of Bruges has gone to bed.

Many venues in Bruges are gay-friendly. The website www.gaybruges.be details addresses of restaurants, bars, hotels and hair salons where gays, lesbians and bisexuals are welcome, as well as all the contacts required to organise a gay wedding, which is legal in Belgium. It also organises regular film nights and social gatherings.

Left: B-In, before the well-dressed masses descend.

33; www.snuffel.be; daily noon–midnight; free; bus: 3, 13; map p.132 B1
A youth hostel bar that attracts locals too, and everyone joins in and enjoys the party at its twice-monthly free live gigs, on the first and third Sat of the month, except July and Aug, starting 9pm.

The Top
Sint-Salvatorskerkhof 5; www.cafethetop.be; Tue–Sat from 9pm, Sun from 10pm; free; bus: 0/Centrum; map p.134 B3
Tiny but lively bar in the lee of the cathedral, where local young people mix with tourists looking for dance sounds in the early hours.

Wereldcafé De Republiek
Sint-Jacobsstraat 36; tel: 050 34 02 29; www.derepubliek.be; daily 11am–2am (earliest); bus: 0/Centrum, 3, 13; map p.134 B4
A more arty crowd comes here to discuss politics, culture and the film they have just seen at the adjacent cinema. A good place to pick up flyers.
SEE ALSO CAFÉS AND BARS, P.35

Gay

Bolero
Garenmarkt 32; tel: 050 33 81 11; Thur–Mon 10pm–late; bus: 1; map p.135 C3
The only dedicated gay bar in town, attracting an older, male crowd.

Cinema

Kinepolis
Koning Albert 1-laan 200; tel: 050 30 50 00; www.kinepolis.com; bus: 7; map p.134 A2
An eight-screen multiplex on the edge of town.

Lumière
Sint-Jacobsstraat 36; tel: 050 34 34 65; www.lumiere.be; bus: 0/Centrum, 3, 13; map p.134 B4
Popular city-centre venue with three screens.

Kaffee L'aMaRaL
Kuipersstraat 10; www.lamaral.be; 9pm–late; free; bus: 0/Centrum; map p.134 B4
DJ slots in this small venue off the Eiermarkt bar circuit are eclectic enough to satisfy all tastes in dance music and draw a friendly crowd of unpretentious young things.

De Lokkedize
Korte Vulderstraat 33; tel: 050 33 44 50; www.lokkedize.be; Wed–Sun from 6pm; bus: 0/Centrum; map p.134 B3
A convivial café attached to a youth hostel that hosts bands playing R&B, as well as jazz, folk and rock. The young crowd show up into the early hours for home-cooked food.

Ma Rica Rokk
't Zand 7–8; tel: 050 33 83 58; www.maricarokk.be; nightly 7pm–4am, Sat–Sun 9pm–6am; free; bus: 0/Centrum; map p.134 A3
Pinball machines, bright-coloured chairs and graffiti murals: the teens' preferred café on 't Zand for a coke and sandwich between classes, and later for partying through the night. The café and terrace are open daily from 7.30am.

Retsin's Lucifernum
Twijnstraat 6–8; tel: 050 34 16 50; Sat 9pm–2am; bus: 0/Centrum; map p.135 C4
Unique venue open just one night a week and serving only rum cocktails: a private house hosting live Latin-American music and flamenco shows. Artist and owner Willy Retsin presides in a place hung with strange paintings and sculptures.

Snuffel Bar
Ezelstraat 47–49; tel: 050 33 31

Below: some drinks are more potent than others.

Painting and Sculpture

The development of oil painting in the early 15th century coincided with the apex of economic prosperity in Bruges. Merchants and nobles who were in the city for business commissioned works by artists and the results were shipped around Europe in a trade that would influence the course of Western art. Over five centuries later, Flanders is rising again as a new force in contemporary art. This section describes the historical movements and artists associated with Bruges, as well as the artists working in Flanders today.

Early Flemish Art

Ever since Charlemagne established his court at Aachen in the 8th century, the artists of the Low Countries had been honing their skills to produce illuminated manuscripts; the culmination was the *Très Riches Heures du Duc de Berry* or Book of Hours (c.1411), by friars from the Flemish province of Limburg. In the early 15th century, these skills were transferred to a larger scale through the use of a new medium: oil paint.

Flemish Primitives

One of the earliest artists to adopt oil painting was **Jan van Eyck** (1390–1441), the first of the so-called Flemish Primitives, who moved to

Bruges in 1425 to cater to the cosmopolitan Dukes of Burgundy. No artist before him had observed nature so minutely, or was capable of rendering observations so precisely – you can visit his *Madonna with Canon George Van der Paele*, in Bruges' Groeningemuseum *(see p.85)*, and the Ghent Altarpiece in Sint-Baafskathedraal *(see p.18)*. Other masters of the time included **Rogier van der Weyden**, **Dirk Bouts** and **Hans Memling**, possibly the only true rival to Van Eyck, whose works for the Sint-Janshospitaal (Memling in Sint-Jan museum; *see p.87*) still hang there today. **Gerard David** is considered to be the last of the Flemish Primitives.

Where once the church had been the main patron of artists, the 15th century saw a rise in secular demand; oil paintings, unlike murals, were portable and marketable. Italian bankers and merchants in Bruges bought Flemish paintings and took them home, where they were greatly admired. Van Eyck painted the *Arnolfini Marriage* (1434) for Giovanni Arnolfini, a merchant from Lucca; the *Portinari Triptych* (1476–78) by Hugo van der Goes was painted for Tommaso Portinari, the Medici family's agent in Bruges. Flemish painters travelled to Italy, and Italian artists adopted oils, shifting away from more labour-intensive mediums.

Below: Khnopff's *Caresses/Art/The Sphinx* (1896) is a classic work of Symbolism.

Left: Memling's *Madonna and Child with two Angels.*

the French movements of Realism, Impressionism and Post-Impression. **Emiel Claus** (1849–1924) created Luminism, based on an Impressionist style.

By the mid-1880s, artists were seeking to express the inner workings of the mind – imagination, emotion, myth and dreams. The term given to this movement was **Symbolism**. North Belgian artists who took up the Symbolist theme included **Leon Spilliaert** (1881–1946) and **Fernand Khnopff** (1858–1921), whose work varies from the realistic to the dreamlike, such as the cheetah with a human head in *Caresses/Art/The Sphinx* (1896; *see* left).

Ostend-born **James Ensor**'s work developed from realism to paintings peopled with skeletons, masks and grotesque cartoon figures. His style anticipated Expressionism by about two decades, and would give rise to the Surrealism of René Magritte (1898–1971) and Paul Delvaux (1897–1994).

Contemporary

In the 1960s, Flemish artists again began to win international recognition. **Marcel Broodthaers** (1924–76) became famous for his iconic mixed-media sculpture *Casserole and Closed Mussels* (1964–65), an amusing take on Pop Art. Installation artist **Panamarenko** (b.1940) produces huge flying machines of PVC, paper, wood and metal; the flat-colour figurative painting of **Luc Tuymans** (b.1958) is widely acclaimed, as is conceptual artist **Wim Delvoye** (b.1965), for his installation *Cloaca* (2000), which imitates the process of food digestion.

Brueghel

Pieter Brueghel the Elder (c.1525–69) travelled to Italy, but his images of Flemish village life – exuberant marriage celebrations in snow-bound winter scenes – are resolutely North European in tone. The charm of Brueghel's work, and that of his son **Brueghel the Younger** (1564–1638), lies in its almost naive directness. Meanwhile, other Flemish painters were acquiring considerable technical skills. **Joachim Beuckelaer** (1533–74), for instance, produced market scenes of astonishing complexity.

Renaissance

After a period of decline in the 16th century, the economic centre of gravity moved to Antwerp – home to **Pieter Paul Rubens** (1577–1640), who restored Flemish art as an international commodity, and his pupil Van Dyck – as well as to the Netherlands, where the first sophisticated market for genre paintings developed. Artists who stayed in Bruges included **Pieter Pourbus** (c.1523–84) from Gouda in

The term 'Flemish Primitives' sounds derogatory, but it relates rather to the original meaning of 'primitive': belonging to the first stage of a new development. The new development in this case was the Renaissance, to which the Primitives were precursors.

Holland, whose style harked back to the Flemish Primitives.

One of the great sculptures of the Renaissance can also be seen in Bruges: the *Madonna and Child* (1506) by **Michelangelo**, which stands in the Onze-Lieve-Vrouwekerk *(see p.47)*.

Independence to Fin-de-siècle

After two centuries of relative anonymity, Belgium greeted independence in 1830 with a renewed search for national and artistic identity. A trend for public statues of historical figures can be seen in **Paul de Vigne**'s (1843–1901) statue of medieval heroes Pieter de Coninck and Jan Breydel on Bruges' Markt *(see p.61)*. Meanwhile, painters echoed

Palaces and Houses

Half of the 10,000 buildings in central Bruges are judged to be of historical value, yet most are not open to the public. This section highlights notable city houses, some built by patricians for their private residence; others – the almshouses dotted around the city – built by the wealthy for the needy and for their own future salvation. Several almshouse gardens and chapels may be entered. Also covered here are a number of abbeys and castles a short distance outside the city and not mentioned elsewhere in this guide.

Abbeys and Castles

Abdij Ter Doest

Ter Doeststraat 4, 8380 Lissewege; tel: 050 54 40 82; www.terdoest.be; daily 10am–7pm; free; bus: 791 or train to Lissewege; map p.139 C4

All that remains of this former Cistercian abbey, destroyed by Dutch rebels in the 16th century, is a remarkable Gothic barn dating from 1250, part of the old farm with pigeon-house (1651) and a monumental entrance gate (1662). The manor farm is now a popular restaurant, Hof ter Doest. Artefacts from the abbey that survived its destruction can be seen in the Lissewege village museum.

SEE ALSO RESTAURANTS, P.120

Fort Beieren

Gemene Wedestraat, Koolkerke; café; tel: 050 67 95 86; www.hippo.be/fort; bus: 4 to Koolkerke Fort Van Beiren; map p.139 D4

Between the village of Koolkerke and the Damme Canal, 4km (2½ miles) north-east of Bruges, this 1702 earthworks fort, and the vestiges of a demolished 19th century

château, are set in what is now a small country park of 26 hectares (64 acres). There is also a car park and café (Wed–Sun 11am–dusk).

Sint-Andriesabdij Zevenkerken

Zevenkerken 4, 8200 Bruges Sint-Andries; tel: 050 40 61 80; www.sint-andriesabdij.org; church: daily, all day except noon–2pm; cafeteria: Sun 10am–7pm, Mon noon–6pm, Tue–Sat 11am–6pm, July–Aug daily until 7pm and Tue–Sat from 10am; free; bus: 72 (stop: Heidelberg; then 1.5km (1 mile) walk along Torhoutsesteenweg back in the direction of Bruges); map p.138 C3

A large Benedictine abbey at Zevenkerken south-west of Bruges on Torhoutsesteen-

> Above the shop-fronts on Steenstraat are some interesting old guildhouses, where details on the facades hint at their former function: at no. 40 is the shoemakers' guildhouse; at no. 38 the joiners' guildhouse; the stonemasons had their headquarters at no. 25; and the bakers at no.19.

weg, founded around 1100 and rebuilt in the 19th century after being destroyed by the Revolutionary French. The abbey is situated amid forests, and the monks run a school and produce fine pottery as well as icons. Only the church is open for day visitors, but there is a cafeteria, the Benediktusheem, serving cheap and cheerful food, and where you can buy the monks' handiwork.

Sint-Trudoabdij Male

Pelderijnstraat 14, 8310 Bruges Sint-Kruis; tel: 050 36 70 20; http://users.skynet.be/abdijmale; entrance charge; Apr–Sept daily 9.30am–noon, 2–6pm, except Wed afternoon, Oct–Mar daily 10am–noon, 2–4pm, except Wed afternoon; bus: 6 (15 min walk) or 58; map p.139 C3

A significant site in the history of Bruges, the St Trudo Abbey of the Sisters of the Holy Sepulchre, situated about 2km (1 mile) east of the Kruispoort city gate, was at one time the Castle of the Counts of Flanders. The 1369 marriage of Margaret, daughter and heir to Lodewijk of Male, to French duke Philip the Bold

Left: castle-turned-abbey, Sint-Trudoabdij Male.

heralded the start of the Burgundian era in Flanders. The original 12th-century castle has been rebuilt and destroyed again by military action or accidental fire throughout the centuries. The vast moated castle-turned-abbey gives a good indication of the power and wealth of the former rulers of Flanders, however, and you can visit the church and the Ridderzaal (Hall of the Knights) in the restored 14th-century keep.

Houses and Palaces

Craenenburg

Markt 16; tel: 050 33 34 02; www.craenenburg.be; daily 7.30am–midnight; bus: 0/Centrum; map p.134 C4

The turreted and crenallated facade of the busy café is all that recalls its past. Once a residence for the Count of Flanders' knights and their lady-folk, its upper floors afforded good views of the jousting tournaments and processions that took place on the Markt. It was in this house that angry Bruges traders held Maximilian of Austria prisoner for 100 days in 1488, after the Hapsburg authorities imposed new taxes. Held behind a barred window in an upper room, he was forced to listen to the torture of his advisers, including Pieter Lanchals, his right-hand man and treasurer. Lanchals had tried to mediate with the insurgents and was executed on the square below Maximilian's window. The hostage-taking of the Crown Prince of the House of Hapsburg, later Emperor Maximilian I, caused a stir across Europe. His father, Emperor Frederick III, dispatched warships and Maximilian was freed, but not before he had been forced to pledge to respect the rights of the burghers of Bruges. He never forgave the city for this episode; as soon as he was freed, he went back on his word and shifted his court to Ghent and the commercial privileges to Antwerp, thus undermining Bruges' importance.

SEE ALSO CAFÉS AND BARS, P.30

Below: little remains of the original Abdij Ter Doest.

Hof Bladelin

Naaldenstraat 19; tel: 050 34 34 83; www.brugge.be/musea; Apr–Sept Mon–Sat 10am–noon, 2–5pm, Sun 10.30am–noon, Oct–Mar Mon–Sat 10am–noon, 2–4pm, Sun 10.30am–noon; free (courtyard only; ring bell to enter); bus: 0/Centrum; 3, 13; map p.132 B1

Only the inner courtyard of this 15th-century mansion can be visited, though the interior, a senior citizens' home, can be seen by appointment. The house was built by Pieter Bladelin (1410–72), who was treasurer to Philip the Good, Duke of Burgundy (the neo-Gothic niche – 1892 – on the outer facade shows Bladelin kneeling before a crowned Madonna and Child). He made a good living: as well as the house, he dabbled in polder reclamation, founded the village of Middelburg, 20km (12 miles) east of Bruges, and was a patron of artists, including Rogier van der Weyden (1399–1464).

Although many are still in use, it is possible to enter the almshouses by pressing the buzzer; you do not need to know the inhabitants.

The Medici Bank of Florence took over the house in 1466, and it is this connection that has given it an Italianate look, including the Renaissance courtyard and ornamental garden, which is thought to be the earliest example of the Renaissance style in the Low Countries. On the courtyard facade are two medallions dating from 1469, depicting Lorenzo de' Medici (Lorenzo the Magnificent) and his wife Clarisse Orsini.

Nearby, at Naaldenstraat 7, is another mansion, **Gistel House**, dating from the end of the 13th century but largely rebuilt in the 16th, by Antoine de Bourbon, Duke of Vendôme. It is now part of the city music conservatory.

Huis Bouchoute

Markt 15; not open to public; bus: 0/Centrum; map p.134 C4

On the opposite corner of Sint-Amandstraat from the Craenenburg café stands this mansion, the Bouchoute House, where the exiled English King Charles II stayed in 1656–57. Dating from 1480, it was restored in 1995 to its original brick Gothic condition. The octagonal compass and weathervane (1682) on the roof allowed merchants to judge their ships' chances of entering or leaving port.

Hof van Watervliet

Oude Burg 27; tel: 050 44 03 77; www.hofvanwatervliet.cm.be; not open to public; bus: 0/Centrum; map p.134 C3

The restored 16th century residence of humanist Marcus Laurinus, Lord of Watervliet (1530–1581). He had many illustrious guests, including Spain's Juan Luis Vives and Erasmus of Rotterdam, who visited frequently

Below: a typical Bruges *godshuis*, or almshouse.

between 1517 and 1521, and was so enthralled by the erudite company he met in Bruges that he called the city the 'Athens of the Low Countries'. English statesman Sir Thomas More, who started writing his political treatise *Utopia* (1515) while in Bruges on official business, was another frequent caller. Together with the house next door – Hof Lanchals (no. 23), once home to Pieter Lanchals, the unlucky advisor to Maximilian of Austria *(see p.99)* – it is now used as offices and a meeting centre for health-related non-profit organisations.

Above: a stained glass detail from Sint-Trudoabdij Male.

Godshuizen

Godshuizen are typical Flemish almshouses, built from the 14th century onwards by wealthy families for the poor, sick or elderly, and by workers' guilds for retired members or their widows. Frequently named after their benefactor, they are of two types: built in a row along a street or clustered around a central garden, with a chapel (where the residents had to pray twice a day for their benefactor's soul) and shared privy, and where each resident was allotted a patch of garden to cultivate. Bruges retains 46 *godshuizen*, containing more than 500 houses, most still used for their original purpose, and allocated to the elderly by the town's social services department. The following list is a pick of the best.

Bouveriestraat
bus: 0/Centrum; map p.134 A2
This street has more almshouses than any other street, several of which have been renovated very recently. At the ramparts end of the street is the **Godshuis**

De Moor (no. 52–76), founded 1480 for retired stonemasons, carpenters and coopers by city magistrate Donaas De Moor, who died in 1483. Next door, at no. 50, **Godshuis Van Volden** occupies the site of a medieval hospital for mentally ill children and foundlings. Near the Zand end of the street are the tiny **Godshuizen Sucx-Van Campen** (1436) and the 17th-century **Godshuis Van Peenen-Gloribus**, which look too small to be inhabited by anyone but a hobbit.

Other former *godshuizen* that have undergone a change in function but which are accessible to the public are the row of cobblers' almshouses that now form the **Bruggemuseum-Volkskunde** (Folklore Museum) at Balstraat 43, and the Adornes family almshouse which is now incorporated into the **Kantcentrum** (Lace Centre), at Peperstraat 3a.
SEE ALSO MUSEUMS AND GALLERIES, P.89

Godshuis De Pelikaan
Groenerei 8; bus: 0/Centrum; map p.135 D4
A small almshouse built 1714 along the now-elegant Groenerei with a beautiful house chapel; see the pelican engraved in the facade.

Godshuizen St Jozef and De Meulenaere
Nieuwe Gentweg 8-22; bus: 1; map p.135 C2
Two of the most accessible: built in the 17th-century around a shared courtyard garden planted with cottage-style flowering beds, and with a tiny chapel and water pump.

Godshuis De Vos
Noordstraat 6–14; bus: 1; map p.134 C2
Eight houses, now converted to six, built 1713 and recently restored, with a smart formal garden and a chapel.

Rooms Convent
Katelijnestraat 9–15; bus: 1; map p.134 C2
The oldest surviving almshouse, built 1330 for women of standing who had chosen to adopt a life of poverty and religious teaching.

101

Pampering

Where better to come for a fashionable chocolate massage than the home of the best chocs in the world? The chocolate used in body treatments is not of the edible variety, however, so licking when the therapist leaves the room is not advised. The Flemings have a complex-free approach to beauty and body care and get themselves groomed and buffed in a no-nonsense manner. The following selection of cosmetic shops, spas and beauty salons is not exhaustive, but reflects the rather modest offering of this mid-sized town; many of the pricier hotels also provide pampering services.

Beauty Institutes

Ann Vandamme

Ezelstraat 55; tel: 050 33 74 07; www.annvandamme.be; Tue 8.30am–8pm, Wed–Sat 8.30am–6.30pm; bus: 3, 13; map p.132 A2

Small beauty institute in town recommended for its use of visibly successful anti-cellulite treatment Ender-mologie, which conducts deep tissue massage and stimulates circulation through suction. The salon specialises in facials, and, for men, Tibetan massage, using warm herbs and hands. There is a small private sauna, too.

Esthetiek Elle

Ezelstraat 147; tel: 050 33 92 59; www.esthetiek-elle.be; Tue–Fri 9am–noon, 1.30–6.30pm, Sat 9am–noon, 1.30–6pm; bus: 3, 13; map p.132 A2

Stylish salon offering seasonal beauty treatment packages (see website for details), as well as chro-matherapy (coloured light) sessions, non-surgical lifting treatment and epilation using IPL (Intense Pulsed Light) technology.

Mixed nudity is the norm in spas (except those in hotels), although swimsuits are sometimes allowed at designated times. Families are welcome.

Cosmetics and Skincare

Ici Paris XL

Noordzandstraat 10; tel: 050 33 73 78; www.iciparisxl.be; Mon–Fri 9.30am–6pm, Sat 9.30am–6.30pm; bus: 0/Centrum; map p.134 B4

Bruges branch of the largest Belgian cosmetics and per-fumery chain, where top scents are traditionally sold at least 20 percent below rec-ommended prices. Helpful, friendly service is its hallmark.

Parfumerie Liberty's

Smedenstraat 23–25; tel: 050 34 36 35; Mon–Fri 10am–6.30pm, Sat 10am–6pm; bus: 0/Centrum; map p.134 A3

Chic perfume and cosmetics store on this smart shopping street, located on the opposite side of 't Zand from the centre, and rarely visited by tourists.

Spas

Fam&Ôm

Heidelbergstraat 49, 8210 Loppem; tel: 050 82 68 63; www.fam-en-om.com; Beauty institute: Mon–Fri 8am–8pm, Sat 8am–6pm; Spa: Mon–Tue 11am–10pm, Fri–Sat 11am–11pm; bus: 74

The principal well-being and beauty centre around Bruges – 7km (4 miles) from the city – which caters for men and women (hence its name) and has a baths complex (mixed, naturist) as well as treatment centre. The owner is known for being rather less than hospitable, but she is the first to admit to this, and has plenty of competent staff to compensate.

The sauna complex has space for 100 people and is well-equipped, with a small pool, Turkish bath and hammam, saunas at 60°, 85° and 100°, outdoor hot tub, plunge pool and foot-bath. Treatments here include Turkish bath body scrub and oil massage, Oriental mud ritual (for couples); and there are also half-day anti-stress packages available for busi-ness clients. Upstairs there is a smart bistro which serves seasonal dishes.

Left: the Sunparks 'Thermae' baths complex.

Smart spa 3km (2 miles) south-west of Bruges, with fluffy dark-grey bathrobes to match the granite floors and flickering fire in the relaxation room. As well as a pool, sauna and hamman, there is a selection of half-day and full-day packages, with options to have a body wrap, mud or hot stone treatment, manicure, pedicure or facial; and of course you can buy luxurious beauty goo on the way out.

Sunparks – Thermae
Sunparks De Haan; Wenduines-teenweg 150; 8420 De Haan; tel: 050 42 95 96; www.sun parks.be; Wed, Sat 11am–2pm (with swimsuit), Tue–Thur, Sat 2–9pm (nude), Sun 2–8pm (nude); coast tram (stop Sun Parks); map p.138 B4

The Sunparks holiday centre near the coast has a 'Thermae' bath complex that is open to the public as well as guests: it has a pool (indoor and outdoor), saunas, Turkish bath, and provides facials and body massages, as well as overnight accommodation deals.

Het Hemelhuis
Groenerei 16; tel: 050 67 96 93; www.hemelhuis.be; Mon–Tue, Thur–Fri 1.30–10.30pm (women only Tue until 4.30pm), Sat 12.30–6pm, June–Aug from 5.30pm Mon–Fri; bus: 0/Centrum; map p.135 D4

The only city-centre bath house, the 'Heaven House' is a stylish sauna and hammam that blends Moorish decor with post-industrial design. As is typical for saunas in Belgium, mixed nudity is the rule, although there is a women-only slot on Tuesdays. A package comprising entry and choice of massage is a treat.

Mozaiek
Dorpsstraat 6, 8200 Sint-Michiels; tel: 050 67 58 07; www.saunabrugge.be; Mon 1–11pm, Tue–Sat 9am–11pm, Sun 5–11pm; bus: 17; map p.138 C3

Pretty but tiny private sauna centre attached to a bathroom store for a maximum of four people, and really intended for two, so must be reserved in advance. It has a Turkish steam bath, sauna, infra-red sauna and a Jacuzzi. Just 4km (2½ miles) from Bruges centre, it is easily accessible

by bus from the city. Special arrangements include a breakfast and champagne package. Tea, coffee, a plate of cakes and fresh fruit are provided free of charge.

Senses
Torhoutsesteenweg 503; 8200 Sint-Michiels; tel: 050 30 05 35; www.senses-wellness.be; Mon–Fri 9am–7pm, Sat 9am–4pm; bus: 25 to Sint-Michiels Vogelzang stop, then 750m/yds walk; map p.138 C3

Below: the Senses spa offers a wide range of treatments.

Parks and Gardens

A small city surrounded by lush farmland, Bruges' parks and gardens tend to be small and perfectly formed. The largest green spaces within the town have always been church property, the gardens of convents and abbeys: the largest is still behind the walls of the seminary of the former Abbey of the Dunes on Potterierei. To glimpse nature in the city, you need simply glance down a lush canal, sit on a café terrace in a tree-lined square or step into a secluded almshouse garden.

Outdoor Spaces

Bruggemuseum-Gezelle Garden

Rolweg 64; tel: 050 44 87 11; www.brugge.be/musea; Tue–Sun 9.30am–12.30pm, 1.30–5pm; bus: 6, 16; map p.133 D1

The museum dedicated to the great Flemish poet and priest (1830–99) in the house that was his birthplace is backed by a pleasant garden, with shady benches and a number of exotic trees and plants.

SEE ALSO MUSEUMS AND GALLERIES, P.90

Graaf Visartpark

Karel de Stoutelaan; bus: 9; map p.132 A1

Situated just outside the city limits in the west, this park takes its name from Count Amedée Visart de Bocarmé (1835–1924), Bruges burgomaster for 50 years from 1876–1924 and a keen advocate of municipal green spaces. It was he who set about transforming the old fortified ramparts into a green boulevard around the city. The park was used as a driving practice ground in the 1960s and there is still a circuit where children can learn the rudiments of the road, as well as a playground and tall trees.

Hof Sebrechts Park

entrances on Beenhouwersstraat and Oude Zak; bus: 9, 41, 42; map p.134 B4

A tranquil oasis hidden behind houses, the Hof Sebrechts (Sebrechts House) park has had a chequered history. It, too, owes its existence to the French demolition of monasteries and convents: this was the vegetable garden of the Sisters of St Elisabeth's Convent, which stood nearby from the 15th century. City archivist Louis Gilliodts-Van Severen and his daughter bought the garden and adjoining 18th-century house in 1885, adding the monumental gate at the Oude Zak entrance in 1907. Surgeon Joseph Sebrechts, who worked at Sint-Janshospitaal, bought the domain in 1928, and hired a landscape architect to create the garden. After he died, the property fell into government hands. Plans to build on it were never realised, and it eventually became a car park. The city finally reopened the garden in 1982. There are benches, a children's play area and sandpit. In summer, the park hosts a sculpture exhibition.

Koning Albertpark

Koning Albertlaan; bus: 0/Centrum; map p.134 B2

A broad strip of green that runs from the station to the 't Zand along the route of the former train line, from when the station was located on the 't Zand square. The garden was developed in the wake of World War II, providing much-needed employment to local men. Today it is

The poplar-shaded courtyard of the Begijnhof de Wijngaarde *(see also Beguinages, p.28)* is one of the most serene and memorable locations in the city, especially in spring when daffodils carpet the lawn. The begijnhof takes its name – Wijngaard – from the vineyard that used to occupy this area, where grapes were grown for making vinegar. Visitors are asked to respect the rule of silence.

Left: a perfectly formed flock of geese on the canal ring park.

popular Queen Astrid, wife of King Leopold III, who died in a road accident in Switzerland with the king at the wheel of their car. The residents of Bruges still call the park 'Botanieken Hof', after its original designation. The park is used for outdoor film screenings during the three-week Klinkers (cobblestones) festival in summer.

Minnewater Park
Minnewater, bus: 1; map p.134 C1

The Minnewater park is dominated by its tree-fringed 'Lake of Love' and the Kasteel

a landscaped green cut-through; and not too disturbed by the ring road to which it runs parallel.

Koningin Astridpark
Minderbroederstraat; bus: 1, 11; map p.135 D3

Koningin Astridpark (Queen Astrid Park) is one of Bruges' largest parks. It has a pond, wrought-iron bandstand (1859), children's playground; even a church, Heilige-Magdelenekerk (Blessed

Mary Magdalene Church), built 1851–3, at the southern end of the park.

Like other green spaces in the city, the park occupies the site of a former monastery; a Franciscan abbey in this case. The land was purchased by the city around 1850 and converted into a botanical garden, becoming a big attraction with Sunday strollers. In 1935 it was given its current name, after the death in 1935 of the

Bruges has a long history of maintaining its green spaces: a letter from Gervatius, Bishop of Reims, dated before 1067 (the year he died) praises the meadows, orchards and vineyards of Bruges, and the fertility of the soil. In the 12th–13th centuries, the city had several Boomgaard (Orchard) streets. The English word 'garden' is derived from the Dutch word for orchard, 'gaard'.

Below: the colourful bandstand in Koningin Astridpark.

Several *godshuizen* (almshouses) in Bruges have attractive, green, inner courtyards. Members of the public may enter when the gate is open; visitors are asked to enjoy the space in silence. Take a look at the 17th-century Godshuizen St Jozef and De Meulenaere on Nieuwe Gentweg, which are built around a courtyard garden with a tiny chapel and water pump *(see also Palaces and Houses, p.101)*.

Above: tranquil Minnewater Park.

Minnewater, a château-style restaurant with a scenic waterside terrace (closed at time of writing). The small garden behind is ideal for a picnic away from the crowds.

The origin of the lake's common name – the 'Lake of Love' – is the source of much debate. French novelist and poet Victor Hugo visited Bruges in 1837 and allegedly christened it the Lac d'Amour. It is said he was inspired by the word *minne*, medieval Dutch for 'love'. But local legend has it that the *minne* was in fact a watery ghost: that of Saxon maiden Minna, who fled the home of her father rather than marry the suitor of his choice. When her lover returned from fighting the Romans, he found her dead of cold and hunger by a stream in the woods. He built a dyke, buried her in the ground, then released the water to create a lake over her resting place. Whatever its origin, the romantic label has stuck and the park is a magnet for dreamy couples. In summer, the park is the venue of the free world music festival Feest in't Park, and the weekend-long Cactus Festival (entrance charge), a rock music event *(see p.92)*.

SEE ALSO CANALS AND BRIDGES, P.41

Ring Canal Park

A long, narrow, green belt around all but the northern perimeter of the city follows the line of the old city ramparts, alongside the ring canal. The remaining four fortified gates of the walls punctuate the route, which can be undertaken on foot or by bicycle. A busy road also traces the ring canal, so it is not the most peaceful place, but it is ideal for a substantial ride, walk or run. The lawns around the windmills in the north-east are popular with sunbathers on fine days.

The park was created over many years, starting in 1876 on the initiative of mayor Count Amedée Visart de Bocarmé *(see p.104)*. Its north-west limit is the Ezelpoort (Donkey Gate). In the south-west, between Smedenpoort and the station, a small brick house in the trees is the Oud Waterhuis (Old Water House), an 18th-century pumping station where a horse-actioned pump was used to extract drinking water, which was then distributed to the various districts. Its origins date back to the 14th century. The gunpowder store of the Poertoren is on the southern tip, beside the Minnewater.

Above: the redbrick lockhouse in Minnewater Park.

The merchants and nobles of medieval Bruges loved their gardens, and made sure that painters included their well-tended plots in artworks they commissioned. *The Legend of St Lucy* triptych (1480) in Sint-Jakobskerk shows an orchard and garden in detail; and the otherwise shocking Gerard David painting in the Groeninge-museum, of the judge being skinned alive, shows a peaceful shady garden in the background *(see also Churches p.48; Museums and Galleries, p.85).*

In the south-east of the park, the recently-added Conzett Brug footbridge across the Coupure means walkers no longer have to make a long detour to reach the opposite bank.

Beyond Bruges

Beisbroek
Zeeweg, Sint-Andries; www.beis broek.be; nature centre: Apr–Nov Mon–Fri 2–5pm, Sun 2–6pm, Mar Sun 2–6pm; planetarium shows: Wed and Sun 3pm and 4.30pm, Fri 8.30pm; during school holi-days also Mon, Tue, Thur 3pm; free (charge for observatory); bus: 52, 53; map p.138 C3

One of two big country estates which stand side by side in the woods just a short distance south-west of Bruges. Beisbroek covers 80 hectares (200 acres), has trees, heathland, footpaths, picnic areas, a deer compound, a cafeteria, a castle that serves as an interactive nature centre, a planetarium and an observatory.

Tudor City Park
Zeeweg, Sint-Andries; tel: 050 32 90 11; daily dawn–dusk; beehives and botanical garden May–Oct Mon–Fri 2–5pm, Sat–Sun 2–6pm; bus: 5; map p.138 C3

Next to Beisbroek, the Tudor City Park covers 40 hectares (100 acres). There is a physic garden, beehives and Tudor-style castle, which is now an upscale restaurant, and reception and conference centre available for hire.

Below: neo-Gothic castle in Tudor City Park dating from 1904–6.

Restaurants

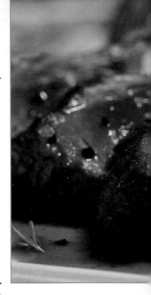

Bruges has a wealth of eateries – from simple cafés to Michelin-starred restaurants – and many excellent addresses within easy walking distance of the Markt and Burg. The city has a tradition of fine feasting and banqueting, and its 21st-century inhabitants uphold this tradition in style. This section recommends a wide choice of restaurants in all price ranges, and includes several addresses for the villages and towns outside Bruges, covered in the Areas chapter of this book. For an introduction to Flemish cuisine, Belgian beers and a description of typical dishes of the region, see 'Food and Drink'.

Markt and Brug

BELGIAN

Breydel – De Coninc
Breidelsstraat 24; tel: 050 33 97 46; €€; Thur–Tue noon–3pm, 6–10pm; bus: 0/Centrum; map p.134 C4
This long-established family-run seafood specialist between the Markt and Burg is the place to eat mussels in Bruges (when in season; expect quite a large portion), as well as lobster and eels. The few street-view tables make it possible to while away an afternoon watching the tourists being trotted away in horse-drawn carriages while indulging in Belgians' preferred pastime: gastronomic indulgence.

Erasmus
Wollestraat 35; tel: 050 33 57 81; www.hotelerasmus.com; €€; Tue–Wed, Fri–Sun noon–4pm, 6–10pm; bus: 1, 11; map p.134 C4

Prices for an average three-course meal with wine:
€ under €25
€€ €25–50
€€€ €50–75
€€€€ over €75

Note that Bruges' restaurants are busy year-round and not just in peak tourist seasons. We advise that you book a restaurant for your evening meal in advance, otherwise you might struggle to find a table on the night.

The modern-styled restaurant in the eponymous hotel is a tippler's dream, with 16 draught beers (the list changes monthly) plus many others in bottles, selected to accompany the food: for example, crown of lamb with parsley and mustard, served with potato and bacon gratin made with Bush blond beer. With less outlandish menus than classy beer-cuisine joint Den Dyver (see p.110), it is also a fair bit cheaper. The menu changes monthly.

Tom Pouce
Burg 17; tel: 050 33 03 36; www.restaurant-tompouce.be; €€; daily 9am–11pm; bus: 0/Centrum; map p.135 C4
This large but not impersonal restaurant enjoys an unrivalled position on the Burg. Although fish and Flemish cuisine dominate the menu, the quality of the food is definitely secondary to that of the location. Order a waffle or pancake, sit on the heated outdoor terrace and watch the world go by.

De Witte Raaf
Hallestraat 4; tel: 050 34 71 29; www.restaurantdewitteraaf.be; €€€; Mon–Wed, Fri–Sat noon–2.30pm, 7–9.30pm; bus: 0/Centrum; map p.134 C4
Rather tucked away down a side street beside the Hallen, the 'White Raven' takes luxurious ingredients on an adventurous journey: duck, foie gras, pigeon, partridge, horse meat and other delectables, some given an Italian twist. There are tables on the sun-trap courtyard to the rear, where the only noise interruptions will be the clanging bells from the Belfry next door.

ITALIAN

Riva del Sole
Wollestraat 22; tel: 050 34 33 30; www.welcome.to/rivadelsole; €€; Thur–Mon noon–2.30pm, 6–10.30pm, Tue noon–2.30pm; bus: 1, 11; map p.134 C4

Left: Bruges restaurants offer plenty of red meat and game.

't Botaniekske
Minderbroedersstraat 26; tel: 050 33 27 90; www.tbotaniekske.be; €; Fri–Sun 6pm–late; bus: 1, 11; map p.135 D3

Friendly neighbourhood restaurant run by an all-female team in a rustic old tavern with a large, cosy fireplace. House specialities include ribs and braised ham, but the menu caters for all tastes and includes fish, frogs legs and vegetarian options among its tapas, wok and pasta dishes. Rather out of the way, but in a green location opposite the children's playground in Koningin Astridpark *(see p.105)*. The service is friendly and the locals love it, which is always good news.

Christophe
Garenmarkt 34; tel: 050 34 48 92; www.christophe-brugge.be; €€–€€€; Thur–Mon 7pm–1am; bus: 1, 11; map p.135 D3

Smoking has been banned in restaurants in Belgium since January 2007. Bars and cafés, however, do not have to respect this rule. Those that serve food must normally have a non-smoking area for this.

close to Minnewater Park, with low beams and a large old brick fireplace. Duck down and tuck in to Belgian staples such as snails in garlic butter, eels in green sauce or *carbonnade fllamande* (beef slow-cooked in beer).

Follow the Italian students from the College of Europe to the place they say does the best pizza in town, and this is where they will take you. The interior decor fulfils all the trattoria clichés – fake climbing vines and bunches of grapes – but you are not here for the setting. The menu makes some concessions to Belgian tastes, but the pizza and pasta dishes are what you come for and are reasonably priced.

South

BELGIAN
Bistro De Bekoring
Arsenaalstraat 55; tel: 050 34 41 57; www.debekoring.be; €€; Tue–Sat noon–2pm, 6.30–9.30pm; Sun noon–2pm; bus: 1; map p.134 C2

Snug and romantic small bistro alongside the canal

Below: Erasmus is located in the hotel of the same name.

Above: a standard tourist menu will feature most local favourites, though quality will vary from place to place.

some little square) specialising in Flemish cuisine. The building, which was formerly the Tanners' Guildhouse, dates from 1630.

Marieke van Brugghe
Mariastraat 17; tel: 050 34 33 66; www.mvb.be; €€; Tue–Sun, café from 8.30am, meals noon–9.30pm, except public holidays; bus: 1; map p.134 C3

Even though it is slap in the middle of tourist-ville, in the shadow of the Onze-Lieve-Vrouwekerk, locals still cherish this restaurant-brasserie-tearoom, which dishes up traditional Flemish fare: rabbit stew, beef cooked in beer and a great fish soup. The terrace for people-watching is an added bonus, but service can be a little frosty. (Do not confuse with the much less loveable place next door: they look like one big establishment.)

Maximiliaan Van Oostenrijk
Wijngaardplein 17; tel: 050 33 47 23; www.maximiliaanvan oostenrijk.be; €€; Thur–Tue 10am–10pm; bus: 1; map p.134 C2

Despite having as touristy a location as you can find in Bruges, adjacent to the Begijnhof and the Minnewater, Maximiliaan's achieves the creditable feat of not being entirely overpowered, but then it does have a lot of tables. Specialities include the traditional local stew, *waterzooi*, grilled meats and seafood.

't Pandreitje
Pandreitje 6; tel: 050 33 11 90; www.pandreitje.be; €€€€; Mon, Tue, Fri, Sat noon–1.30pm,

Definitely worth leaving the beaten track (but not by too far) for an excellent dining experience at this unpretentious 'evening and night bistro'. The chef has won fans far and wide for his excellent way with no-nonsense staples, available till late into the night.

Den Dyver
Dijver 5; tel: 050 33 60 69; www.dyver.be; €€€; Fri–Tue noon–2pm, 6.30–9pm; bus: 0/Centrum; map p.134 C3

Be prepared for an adventure in taste at this family-run house renowned for inventive beer cuisine that contrasts with the more typical Flemish beer-recipes such as *carbonnade fllamande*. All dishes – like duck breast with guinea fowl and mint mousse in a Chimay sauce with caramelised figs, and peach and chicory stew – come

accompanied by selected Belgian brews; desserts are prepared with local genever. Not cheap, but unique.

De Gastro
Braambergstraat 6; tel: 050 34 51 24; www.degastro.be; €–€€; Thur–Tue 11am–11pm; bus: 6, 16; map p.135 C4

This stylish address has concocted a menu to please all comers, from snacks to Belgian classics and fusion-inspired dishes, while pancakes and waffles are served all afternoon. Prices are lower than the decor and smart presentation suggest.

't Huidevettershuis
Huidenvettersplein 10–11; tel: 050 33 95 06; www.huidevettershuis.be; €€; Mon, Wed–Fri noon–2pm, 7–10pm, Sat–Sun noon–10pm; bus: 0/Centrum; map p.135 C4

An elegant canal-side eatery (with an entrance on a hand-

Prices for an average three-course meal with wine:
€ under €25
€€ €25–50
€€€ €50–75
€€€€ over €75

Above: 't Pandreitje's chef takes time out from his busy kitchen.

Belgium has two Michelin three-starred restaurants: the Hof van Cleve in Kruishotem, not far from Ghent, and De Karmeliet in Bruges *(see p.118)*.

De Visscherie
Vismarkt 8; tel: 050 33 02 12; www.visscherie.be; €€€€; Wed–Mon noon–2pm, 7–10pm, closed early December; bus: 0/Centrum; map p.135 C4
The subtle flavours of the sea are cooked to absolute perfection in this top-notch fish and seafood restaurant, situated right on the fish market (Vismarkt). A formal establishment where the mâitre d' will attend to your every whim, this is ideal for a special occasion with all the frills. A few meat dishes are also available.

De Wijngaert
Wijngaardstraat 15; tel: 050 33 69 18; www.wijngaert.com; €; daily noon–3pm, 6–10pm, café service from 11am; closed Wed and Thur in winter; bus: 1; map p.134 C2

7–9pm; bus: 1, 6; map p.135 C3
Elegant and refined Franco-Belgian cuisine is served in spacious comfort in this Renaissance-era patrician house near the Rozenhoed-kaai. Chef Guy Van Neste runs the kitchen and wine cellar, while his English-born wife welcomes guests. The seafood is excellent.

Salade Folle
Walplein 13–14; tel: 050 34 94 43; www.saladefolle.com; €; Thur–Mon 11.30am–9.30pm, Tue 11.30am–3pm; bus: 1; map p.134 C2
This bright, contemporary café and tearoom serves good soups, salads, quiches and pasta in generous portions (the pasta dishes are rather average but the rest is good). Rustic blond wood tables are divided over two floors with a mezzanine. Good for vegetarians and lone diners.

Below: restaurant Maximiliaan Van Oostenrijk succeeds in providing quality Belgian food in a tourist-friendly setting.

Above: unsurprisingly, Salade Folle specialises in salads.

No-frills, friendly service assured at this grill restaurant, bar and tearoom along the well-worn tourist groove between the Beguinage and Onze-Lieve-Vrouwekerk. Well-prepared mussels, ribs and a lot more besides, but especially worth a stop for the house-speciality: sangría, made with red or white wine.

't Zwaantje
Gentpoortvest 70; tel: 0473 71 25 80; www.hetzwaantje.be; €€€; Fri–Tue noon–2pm, 6.30–10pm; bus: 1; map p.135 C1

If you have come to Bruges to indulge in romantic fantasies, this venue could be the icing on the cake, with its Tiffany-style lamps, mirrors, and candlelight. A local treasure that tourists have never really discovered, run by a welcoming family down near the Bargehuis off Katelijnestraat. Belgian-French cuisine is lovingly presented and served. The chef's chocolate desserts have won multiple awards, too.

FRENCH
Couvert
Eekhoutstraat 17; tel: 050 33 37 87; www.couvert-brugge.be; €€–€€€; Thur–Mon noon–2pm, 6–10pm; bus: 1, 11; map p.134 C3

Loving attention to French-influenced cuisine, service and presentation have earned this slightly back-street address a faithful following. The fixed price menu is inventive and seasonal – gratin of scallops and asparagus; baked guinea fowl with stuffed mushrooms and creamy parsley sauce – while the à la carte is brief but diverse. Romantic setting with white-dressed tables and brick-exposed walls.

Den Gouden Harynck
Groeninge 25; tel: 050 33 76 37; www.goudenharynck.be; €€€€; Tue–Fri noon–2pm, 7–9pm, Sat 7–10.30pm, closed last week of Dec, one week at Easter, end July–mid-Aug; bus: 1; map p.134 C3

Formal haven of top-notch modern French gastronomy in a 17th-century former fishmonger's behind Groeningemuseum. Chef Philippe Serruys stamps his flair on sensuous creations such as smoked lobster with fig and date chutney, Muscovite potato and Sevruga caviar. Eating here is a seriously luxurious experience.

Duc de Bourgogne
Huidenvettersplein 12; tel: 050 33 20 38; www.ducdebourgogne.be; €€€; Tue 7–9.30pm, Wed–Sun noon–2.30pm, 7–9.30pm; bus: 0/Centrum; map p.135 C4

A classic dining experience, with French-style dishes in beautiful surroundings and a canal view. Sup like a lord on lobster and roast meat in rich sauce among the artworks and tapestries. Good-value, all-inclusive menus, especially for lunch.

Malesherbes
Stoofstraat 3-5; tel: 050 33 69 24; €; Wed–Sun noon–1.45pm, 7–9pm; bus: 1; map p.134 C2

The all-female team is a winning combination in this simply decorated French deli and dining room in the so-called narrowest street in Bruges. With famously attentive service and a good atmosphere, it serves quality French produce, quiches and regional specialities. The deli is open from 10am.

INDIAN
Indian Tandoori
Oude Gentweg 11; tel: 050 34 58 26; www.indiantandoori.be; €–€€; Wed–Mon noon–2.30pm, 6–11pm; bus 1; map p.134 C2

Prices for an average 3 course meal with wine:
€ under €25
€€ €25–50
€€€ €50–75
€€€€ over €75

> The restaurants on the Markt are firmly aimed at the passing tourist trade and none are worthy of particular recommendation. Their terraces are fine for a drink and a view, but avoid dining here if you want to get good quality food for a reasonable price.

Although right in the heart of the tourist zone, this modest but excellent Indian restaurant is just off the main drag and so often overlooked. Seek it out for subtly spiced, authentic dishes from the sub-continent, made with the freshest ingredients and served with understated grace.

VEGETARIAN
De Bron
Katelijnestraat 82; tel: 050 33 45 26; €; Tue–Sat 11.45am–2pm; bus: 1; map p.134 C2
Locals pack in to this spotless lunch-only restaurant with an atrium at rear which opens in fine weather. You join a table wherever there is a seat and eat the day's soup or its one dish: a mixed platter that might include a gratin, a grain, and baked, steamed and raw vegetables (just choose small, medium or large; vegan option on request). The locals use it rather like an unofficial canteen and get talking to whoever they sit with. No tourists guaranteed; you have to ring the bell to get in, but once in the staff are very friendly. Take-out service of the day's menu is also available.

FUSION
De Stoepa
Oostmeers 124; tel: 050 33 04 54; www.stoepa.be; €; Tue–Sun 11am–late; bus: 0/Centrum; map p.134 B1
Sociable hangout near the station popular for its informal atmosphere and cuisine with an Oriental twist. Vegetarian-friendly and as good for a drink and a nibble as a proper tuck-in. The walled terrace-garden is a fantastic sun trap on fine days.

West
BELGIAN
Aneth
Marie van Bourgondiëlaan 1; tel: 050 31 11 89; www.aneth.be; €€€€; Tue–Fri noon–2pm, 7–9pm, Sat 7–9pm; bus: 9; map p.132 A1

Local foodies who like their fish adore Aneth and book ahead to celebrate special occasions. The roomy detached house beside the Graaf Visartpark outside the ring road is well off the tourist circuit and worth the trip for top-class preparations of the day's catch, fresh from the coast and presented in style.
Cafedraal
Zilverstraat 38; tel: 050 34 08 45; www.cafedraal.be; €€€; Mon–Sat noon–3pm, 6–11pm; bus: 0/Centrum; map p.134 B3
Impressive collection of 15th-century buildings given a contemporary makeover for fashionable dining (seafood is its speciality) on two floors and on its large back garden-terrace. Colin Farrell's character caused a scene here in *In Bruges*. Open for drinks only from 3–6pm.
Chagall
Sint-Amandsstraat 40; tel: 050 33 61 12; €; Thur–Tue 11am–11pm; bus: 0/Centrum; map p.134 B4
Whether you are out for a few drinks or for a heart-warming pot of mussels in cream sauce, you may have to fight for a table on this popular

Below: family-run 't Zwaantje is a local favourite.

bistro's terrace, which is perfect for people-watching and afternoon sun on the pedestrianised Sint-Amandsstraat. Classical music plays in the cosy interior, which has an open hearth, wooden beams and stained-glass windows.

Grand Café De Passage

Dweersstraat 26; tel: 050 34 02 32; www.passagebruges.com; €; bar 5pm–midnight and later, restaurant 6–11pm; bus: 0/Centrum; map p.134 B3

Absolutely the best cheap eat in town; long brown café in *belle-époque* style packed with tables. Locals love it and there is a youth hostel upstairs, so an atmosphere is guaranteed every night. Good for ribs and grilled food, served with either jacket potatoes or chips.

De Hobbit

Kemelstraat 8; tel: 050 33 55 20; www.hobbitgrill.be; €€; Mon, Wed–Sat noon–2pm, 6–11pm, Sun 6–11pm; bus: 0/Centrum; map p.134 B3

Popular and reasonably-priced ribs and grilled food restaurant – 'Middle Earth cuisine', they claim – across the street from renowned beer joint 't Brugs Beertje *(see p.33)*. The decor is dark and rustic, with low ceilings and antique kitchen implements.

Kardinaalshof

Sint-Salvatorskerkhof 14; tel: 050 34 16 91; www.kardinaalshof.be; €€€; Fri–Tue noon–2.15pm, 7–9.15pm, Thur 7–9.15pm; bus: 0/Centrum; map p.134 B3

Comfort, elegance and fine dining reign supreme in this smart town house just behind Sint-Salvatorskathedraal,

Prices for an average three-course meal with wine:
€ under €25
€€ €25–50
€€€ €50–75
€€€€ over €75

Right: Cafedraal sells modern seafood in a revitalised 15th-century setting.

where the focus is on seafood. The bright upholstery and fixed monthly menu (with or without accompanying wines) lends an atmosphere rather like that of a private dining room. This restaurant is not a good choice for small appetites: count on five or six courses for the evening meal, three plus at lunchtime. A 'special occasion' favourite.

De Koetse

Oude Burg 31; tel: 050 33 76 80; www.dekoetse-brugge.be; €€; Fri–Wed noon–2.30pm, 6–10pm; bus: 0/Centrum; map p.134 C3

This inviting restaurant has a rustic Flemish interior with a blazing fire in winter. It serves robust Flemish cooking, including North Sea fish dishes, spare ribs and excellent *frites*.

De Mangerie

Oude Burg 20; tel: 050 33 93 36; www.mangerie.com; €€€; Tue–Sat noon–1.30pm, 7–9pm; bus: 0/Centrum; map p.134 C3

The young couple who run this restaurant have gained a reputation for their scrummy dishes and painstaking presentation – and a short menu featuring a starter and main course from each of four styles: 'refreshed classic', 'funky new style', Mediterranean and vegetarian; dishes are along the lines of filet of venison with juniper berries and Jerusalem artichoke sauce; and pike perch with aubergine caviar, tomatoes and chorizo oil.

Patrick Devos

Zilverstraat 41; tel: 050 33 55 66; www.patrickdevos.be; €€€€; Mon–Fri noon–1.30pm, 7–9pm, Sat 7–9pm; bus: 0/Centrum; map p.134 B3

Star chef and wine-taster Devos gives his name to this chic-as-they-come temple to gastronomy in the historic 'Zilveren Pauw' (Silver Peacock) house, formerly the second residence of the abbot of Ghent cathedral. The 13th-century gabled frontage contrasts with the stunning art nouveau interior, the result of a late 19th-century makeover that gives the impression of dining in a private club. The menu draws on fresh regional produce, complemented by suitably top-class wines.

't Putje

't Zand 31; tel: 050 33 28 47; www.hotelputje.be; €€; daily 8.30am–11pm; bus: 0/Centrum; map p.134 B3

Facing the Concertgebouw, the crisp tablecloths and smart wicker armchairs set this large, popular hotel brasserie apart from the nearby run-of-the-mill pavement cafés on the 't Zand. Reasonably priced and good French and Belgian classics are served round the clock.

De Stove

Kleine Sint-Amandsstraat 4; tel: 050 33 78 35; www.restaurant destove.be; €€€; Sat–Tue noon–1.30pm, 7–9.30pm, Fri 7–9.30pm, closed two weeks in Jan, two weeks in June; bus: 0/Centrum; map p.134 B4

Homely and intimate De Stove specialises in Flemish cuisine with the emphasis on salad, fish and steaks. Mouthwatering scallops on black pasta with tomato tapenade, and sea bream with couscous, stuffed aubergine and basil oil are just some of the pleasingly original menu items in this unfussy, intimate 20-seater, set in an old gabled house. At the lower end of this price bracket

FRENCH

Guillaume

Korte Lane 20; tel: 050 34 46 05; www.guillaume2000.be; €€€; Wed–Sun noon–2pm, 7–11pm, except Sat lunch; bus: 9; map p.134 A4

Bijou, whitewashed cottage on a terraced street off the tourist circuit near the t' Zand. Houses a popular, high-quality bistro run by owner-chef Wim Vansteelant. The menu includes a small but tasty selection of starters and main courses with a distinct Franco-Belgian flavour, such

as mackerel stuffed with Liège potatoes and mustard ham.

INDIAN

Bhavani

Simon Stevinplein 5; tel: 050 33 90 25; www.bhavani.be; €€; Thur–Tue noon–2.30pm, 6–10pm; bus: 0/Centrum, 1; map p.134 B3

Quality and authentic Indian cuisine – including vegetarian – served in stylish surroundings. Madras and tandoori dishes are specialties. The set lunch on weekdays is good value.

SPANISH

Bodega Lorena's

Loppemstraat 13; tel: 050 34 88 17; €€; Tue–Sat noon–2.30pm, 6–9pm; bus: 0/Centrum, 1; map p.134 B3

Spanish restaurant (not a bar) on a tiny alley off Simon Stevinplein, which does

Below: De Koetse serves hearty Flemish specialties.

authentic Iberian cuisine – a large selection of tapas, plus paella – in a dining room unchanged since the 1970s.

VEGETARIAN

De Zen

Beenhouwersstraat 117; tel: 050 33 67 02; €; Mon–Fri noon–2pm; bus: 9; map p.132 A1

A wholesome and varied dish-of-the-day is all that is on the menu besides soup in this vegan-friendly lunch restaurant. Its forte is macrobiotic cuisine, so expect soya and seaweed aplenty.

North

BELGIAN

Brasserie Forestière

Academiestraat 11; tel: 050 34 20 02; www.brasserieforestiere.be; €; Mon, Tue, Thur 11.30am–6pm, Fri–Sat 11.30am–3pm, 6–10pm; bus: 4, 14; map p.132 C1

Reasonably priced, popular and laid-back diner in an elegant town house with marble fireplaces and scrubbed pine tables. Light meals – pasta, quiche, salads, desserts – are served by friendly staff. Caters for vegetarians.

If you fancy immersing yourself in medieval Bruges, or have a family to entertain, try **Brugge Anno 1468** (Vlamingstraat 86; tel: 050 34 75 72; www. celebrations-entertainment.be; Apr–Oct Fri–Sat, Nov–Mar Sat only, doors 7pm for show 7.30–10.15pm; bus: 3, 13; map p.132 C1.) A theme dinner venue in a former church, you can sup in Burgundian style while jesters, minstrels, dancers, falconers and fire-eaters recreate the 1468 wedding feast of Charles the Bold and Margaret of York. Various price packages available. Reduced for under-15s (free for under-6s). Advise two days ahead if vegetarian food required.

Above: fondue and other Belgian classics are served at Pietje Pek.

Brasserie Souffleur

Vlamingstraat 58; tel: 050 34 82 92; www.souffleur.be; €€; Fri–Wed 11am–11pm; bus: 0/Centrum; map p.134 C4

Brisk and smart brasserie for good snacks and salads across the road from the Stadsschouwburg (city theatre), with a warming open hearth in winter and a sunny terrace streetside in summer. Excellent mussels and chips; afternoon tea served 2–6pm.

Curiosa

Vlamingstraat 22; tel: 050 34 23 34; www.curiosa-brugge.com; €€; Tue–Fri noon–3pm, 6–10.30pm, Sat noon–11pm, Sun noon–10pm; bus: 0/Centrum; map p.134 C4

Cellar tavern with a vaulted ceiling and brick walls. Surprisingly tourist-free despite its proximity to the Markt, it serves a broad range of Belgian classics, including salads, steaks and seafood specialities. Spacious enough for larger groups.

't Oud Handbogenhof

Baliestraat 6; tel: 050 33 19 45; €€; Tue–Sat 6–10pm, Sun noon–1.30pm, 6–10pm; bus: 4, 14; map p.133 C2

Wonderful 'olde worlde' place in peaceful Sint-Gillis neighbourhood peopled by characters from Brueghelian paintings. Flagstones, wooden beams, gigantic fire-

place, heavy oak furniture, and a hearty no-nonsense approach to solid Belgian cuisine – from steak, fish or mussels to snacks like omelettes and toasted sandwiches. The garden to the rear is shady in fine weather. Not a lot of tourists open the heavy door to step inside, and they are missing out.

Au Petit Grand

Philipstockstraat 18; tel: 050 34 86 71; www.aupetitgrand.be; €€; Tue–Sun 6pm–midnight; bus: 0/Centrum; map p.134 C4

Fuel up after a day's hard sightseeing on T-bone steak or rack of lamb at this pretty and popular address for grilled fish and meat specialities. It is not enormous and the locals like it here, so reservation is advised.

Pietje Pek

Sint-Jakobsstraat 13; tel: 050 34 78 74; www.pietjepek.com; €€; Thur–Tue from 5.30pm; bus: 0/Centrum; map p.134 B4

Behind its art nouveau facade, this traditional (and unashamedly tourist-focused) restaurant serves up satisfying portions of its speciality cheese and meat fondues, as well as a limited menu of hearty Belgian classics.

Zeno

Vlamingstraat 53; tel: 050 68 09 93; www.restaurantzeno.be; €€; Tue–Fri noon–2pm, 7–9pm,

Sat 7–9pm; bus: 3, 13; map p.132 C1

Run by a couple of young perfectionists, this new venture has a monthly menu composed of eight courses from which you can select four to seven, or else a faster lunch option. The presentation is ravishing, and the Franco-Belgian cuisine excellent; but if you loathe nouvelle cuisine this place is not for you.

AFRICAN
Baobab
Philipstockstraat 27; tel: 050 33 14 08; www.bistrobaobab.be; €€; Tue–Sun noon–1.15pm, 6.30–10pm, 11pm at weekends, no lunch Saturday; bus: 0/Centrum; map p.134 C4

A welcome recent addition to the Bruges restaurant scene,

> Prices for an average three-course meal with wine:
> € under €25
> €€ €25–50
> €€€ €50–75
> €€€€ over €75

this cheerful South African bistro serves mouthwatering dishes enhanced with spices, coconut milk and other flavours of sunnier climes, washed down, as you would expect, with wines of the region. The meat (springbok, ostrich) and fish (tilapia, tiger prawns) are imported direct from South Africa. (What about carbon footprints?) There are lots of veggie options, and the friendly owner will also cater to gluten- or lactose-intolerance if requested.

Below: mussels and chips served with the obligatory beer at pristine Brasserie Souffleur

EUROPEAN
De Florentijnen
Academiestraat 1; tel: 050 67 75 33; www.deflorentijnen.be; €€€; Tue–Sat noon–2.30pm, 6.30–10.30pm; bus: 3, 4, 13, 14; map p.132 C1

Stylish eatery set in a modern retake of a medieval interior. It has a lively buzz and dishes up superb Italian-French food, with painstaking attention to presentation. Credit cards accepted for sums over €100 only.

FRENCH
Chez Olivier
Meestraat 9; tel: 050 33 36 59; €€€–€€€€; Mon–Wed, Fri noon–1.30pm, 7–9.30pm, Sat 7–9.30pm; bus: 0/Centrum; map p.135 C4

Impeccable all-white dining room overlooking the most romantic stretch of canal in Bruges. A peaceful and resolutely elegant upmarket choice, set in a beautiful 16th-century building with meat-focused, refined French-Belgian flavours on the menu.

In Den Wittenkop
Sint-Jakobsstraat 14; tel: 050 33 20 59; €€; Tue–Fri noon–2pm, 6–9.30pm, Sat 6–9.30pm; bus: 0/Centrum; map p.134 B4

Mellow café-bistro lined with retro enamel advertising panels and run by a stylish and friendly couple. Although it describes its cuisine as French, the menu includes Belgian standards such as *waterzooï* – made with langoustines rather than white fish or chicken. Lush terrace to the rear.

FUSION
Tom's Diner
West Gistelhof 23; tel: 050 33 33 82; www.tomsdiner.be; €€; Wed–Mon 6–11pm; bus: 3, 13; map p.132 C2

Convivial gem highly popular with locals in an unprepos-

117

sessing neighbourhood, with a candlelit setting and exposed brick walls, so nothing like a diner in the commonly understood sense. Blends Belgian dishes with international influences to successful effect.

ITALIAN
Trium Trattoria
Academiestraat 23; tel: 050 33 30 60; www.trattoriatrium.be; €; Tue–Sun 9am–9pm; bus: 4, 14; map p.132 C1

Authentic Italian deli, take-out and eaterie in the old merchants' quarter where their compatriots once came to trade; this is the real thing, with home-made pasta and all the best produce from Italy. The deli counter and shop side sells wines, pasta, cheeses and hams.

VEGETARIAN
Lotus
Wapenmakersstraat 5; tel: 050 33 10 78; www.lotus-brugge.be; €; Mon–Sat 11.45am–2pm; bus: 0/Centrum; map p.135 C4

Popular and long-established 'natural' restaurant that serves lunches only. Very good value for the carefully prepared dishes using hormone-free meat in the daily dish of either lamb moussaka or lamb stew, plus vegetarian options.

East
BELGIAN
Bistro De Schaar
Hooistraat 2; tel: 050 33 59 79; €€; Fri–Wed noon–2.30pm, 6–10pm; bus: 6, 16; map p.135 E4

This rustic bistro, with a pavement terrace beside the Coupure yacht harbour, provides an entirely different experience to city-centre restaurants that are generally full of tourists. A popular and friendly neighbourhood eatery, with an open grill-fire,

it serves fish and meat dishes. Locals reserve tables so it is wise to do the same.

Bistro Refter
Molenmeers 2; tel: 050 44 49 00; €€–€€€; Tue–Sat L & D; bus 6, 16; map p.135 D4

Opened early 2009, this new venture of Geert Van Hecke (chef of De Karmeliet, *see above*) brings his culinary magic within the reach of mere mortals, and spares them the pomp and ceremony of the main restaurant – 'refter' means refectory. Dishes are variations on the bistro standards: asparagus served every which way; snails, fish soup, scallops and so on; the wine list is good and seating comfortable if not spacious. Reserve well in advance: everyone wants a piece of the superstar chef at a fraction of the usual price.

Ganzespel
Ganzenstraat 37; tel: 050 33 12 33; www.ganzespel.be; €; Fri–Sun 6.30–10.30pm; bus: 6, 16; map p.135 D4

Small ancient house on a residential street with a bed and

breakfast upstairs and homely feel downstairs, very reasonably priced daily menu comprises soup, salad, main course and beer, a choice of which will be explained by welcoming owner Nicky. Recommended for those on a tight budget.

In 't Nieuw Museum
Hooistraat 42; tel: 050 33 12 80; www.nieuwmuseum.com; €€; daily 11am–2pm, 6–10pm, except Wed eve and Sat lunch; bus: 6, 16; map p.135 E4

A simple front room in a humble terraced house, decorated like an old brown café festooned with dried hops and with a roaring open fire. It serves home-cooked Belgian favourites including eels in green sauce, grilled prawns and mussels (in season), a variety of grilled meats, and simple oven-baked dishes such as lasagne, for no-frills dining with a warm-heart. Good beer selection and changing beer of the month.

De Karmeliet
Langestraat 19; tel: 050 33 82 59; www.dekarmeliet.be;

Below: an impressive array of cheeses are available at Trium Trattoria's deli counter.

€€€€; Tue–Sat noon–3pm, 6–11pm, plus Easter and Whit Sunday; bus: 6, 16; map p.135 D4

Step off uninspiring Langestraat through the great double doors and and enter a world of jaw-dropping culinary creations in grand surroundings. A legend beyond Belgium's borders, De Karmeliet occupies a gastronomic class of its own, thanks to the genius of indefatigable owner-chef Geert Van Hecke. At the time of writing, one of just two three-star Michelin restaurants in Belgium.

De Nisse
Hooistraat 12; tel: 050 34 86 51; €€; Wed–Sun 6–10pm, Sat–Sun noon–2.30pm; bus: 6, 16; map p.135 E4

Homely fondu specialist that also has a varied beer selection. Good hearty soups, garlicky prawns and seasonal specialities. Although slightly out of the way and doing little to publicise itself, it has established a faithful following.

FRENCH
Rock Fort
Langestraat 15; tel: 050 33 41 13; www.rock-fort.be; €€€; Mon–Fri 12.30–2pm, 6.30–11pm; bus: 6, 16; map p.135 D4

Diminutive fashionable bistro with a simple formula: good food – French with fusion influences – generous portions and stylish decor. Seating may be on bar stools so specify if this is not acceptable.

Sans Cravate
Langestraat 159; tel: 050 67 83 10; www.sanscravate.be; €€€; Tue–Fri noon–2pm, 7–9.30pm, Sat 7–9.30pm; bus: 6, 16; map p.135 D4

The self-styled 'cooking theatre', due to the open kitchen in the middle of the

Above: Koto's sushi is freshly prepared and delicious.

room, does original and super-stylish food in a decor to match. The characterful owner divides opinion between those who love him and those who hate him, but his culinary pedigree is unquestionable and the food – spit roasts a speciality – is guaranteed to win over all your senses.

JAPANESE
Koto
Potterierei 15; tel: 050 44 31 31; www.hoteldemedici.com; €€€; Tue–Sun 7–10pm, Sun noon–2pm; bus: 4, 14; map p.133 D2

Japanese food in stylish surroundings, in the Hotel Medici. Meat is tender and savoury, vegetables have just the right degree of crunchiness, sushi and sashimi seafood is fresh and bright, and the sake is warm. Teppan yaki grilled meat and fish are the speciality.

> Prices for an average three-course meal with wine:
> € under €25
> €€ €25–50
> €€€ €50–75
> €€€€ over €75

Damme
BELGIAN
De Damse Poort
Kerkstraat 29; tel: 050 35 32 75; www.damsepoort.be; €€; Thur–Tue 10am–10pm; map p.139 D2

A smart old farmhouse with an elegant dining room plus a large back garden for fine weather, serving Flemish staples with a seafood bent – eels, oysters, shrimps and sole – and teas between meals.

Tante Marie
Kerkstraat 38; tel: 050 35 45 03; www.tante-marie.be; €; Sat–Thur 10am–6pm; map p.139 C3

Delightful tearoom and lunch restaurant serving light meals. Try the three-ingredients fish dish to sample the specialities of the region: tomato stuffed with shrimps, shrimp croquette, etc. The dining room is decorated in country-style with lots of natural wood and there is a terrace for fine weather. Absolutely wicked pastries and cakes, and a fixed-price lunch menu with champagne on weekdays.

Above: Hof ter Doest's seasonal menu includes fresh game in autumn.

Lissewege

BELGIAN

Danny Horseele
Stationsweg 45c, Lissewege-Dudzele; tel: 050 32 10 32; www.dannyhorseele.be; €€€€; Mon–Tue, Thur–Sat noon–2pm, 7–9.30pm; bus: 42 to Dudzele then walk; map p.139 C4

Chef Horseele was awarded two Michelin stars in 2009 for his latest venture, located in a farmhouse between Lissewege and Dudzele which even has its own heliport. His top-notch gastronomy employs luxurious ingredients in complex preparations with prices to match: choose from à la carte, fixed-price tasting menu or special lunch menu.

Hof ter Doest
Ter Doeststraat 4; tel: 050 54 40 82; www.terdoest.be; €€; daily noon–3pm, 5–9pm; café: daily 9am–midnight and later; train to Lissewege then walk; map p.139 C4

Prices for an average three-course meal with wine:
€ under €25
€€ €25–50
€€€ €50–75
€€€€ over €75

In a sprawling farm that rose from the ruins of the former Ter Doest Cistercian Abbey, this large, family-friendly restaurant with a vast terrace combines the hallowed qualities and fresh produce of its predecessors in an elegant country setting. Sample North Sea specialities – eels, shrimps, oysters and lobster – or a wide selection of game dishes in autumn.

Ghent

BELGIAN

De Blauwe Zalm
Vrouwebroersstraat 2; tel: 09 224 08 52; www.deblauwezalm.be; €€€; Tue–Fri L & D, Sat and Mon D only; tram: 1, 4 (stop: Sint-Veerleplein); map p.136 C4

A go-to address for gastronomes in the hip Patershol district; 'The Blue Salmon' is renowned for inventive fish and seafood. Instead of formulaic standards, its concoctions use local specialities like asparagus, Oriental spices or Mediterranean herbs, served in a stylish modern interior or on the garden terrace.

Brasserie HA'
Kouter 29; tel: 09 265 91 81;

www.brasserieha.be; €€–€€€; Mon–Sat noon–2.30pm, 6–10pm, Sun 9–11.30am; tram: 1 (stop: Korte Meer); map p.136 C3

Elegant yet cool, the Handelsbeurs Theatre's café-restaurant serves refined but not too high-brow French and Belgian cuisine – light and breezy for lunch, candle-lit romantic for dinner – to foodies and theatregoers alike. A fantastical multi-coloured modern chandelier graces the main dining room, and in the summer you can enjoy your meal seated on the lovely outside terrace overlooking the Ketelvaart canal.

EUROPEAN

Le Grand Bleu
Snepkaai 15; tel: 09 220 50 25; www.legrandbleu.be; €€€; daily 11.30am–5.30pm (kitchen until 2.30pm), 6.30pm–1am (kitchen until 9pm); bus: 34; map p.136 C4

Set in a small Provençal-style house with a lovely terrace by the Leie, west of Sint-Pietersstation, this seafood specialist presents Mediterranean-influenced fish dishes and a wide range of lobster variations. A few succulent meat dishes are also on offer.

VEGETARIAN
Eethuis Avalon
Geldmunt 32; tel: 09 224 37 24; www.restaurantavalon.be; €; Mon–Sat 11.30am–2.30pm, plus first Fri of month 7–9pm for special four-course menu; tram: 1 (stop: Gravensteen); map p.136 B4

Across the street from the Gravensteen, Avalon is a far cheerier medieval reference. Among its informal organic-vegetarian concoctions, home-made soup served with home-baked bread, followed by a slice of savoury quiche seems like lordly fare. The antique-tiled main room is a protected monument; there is also a charming small garden terrace.

De Warempel
Zandberg 8; tel: 09 224 30 62; www.dewarempel.be; €–€€; Mon–Fri 11.45am–2pm, except public holidays; bus: 55; map p.137 C3

The menu at this lunch restaurant and local favourite comprises a one-dish mixed platter, with optional soup starter and dessert. The custom, if you do not book, is to join a table with other diners.

De Haan

BELGIAN
Strand Hotel
Zeedijk 19; tel: 059 23 34 25; www.strandhotel-dehaan.be; €€; Thur–Tue 11am–9pm; coast tram (stop: De Haan aan Zee); map p.138 B4

Comfortable hotel-restaurant with a prime position on the promenade. The glazed

> For seafood fresh off the boat, head to Ostend's Visserskaai where stalls and restaurants deal directly with the fishing fleet.

veranda area is better than the rather soulless dining room inside, and you get a sea view, sunset included, on a good day. Weekly fixed menu and staples like sole, mussels and frogs' legs.

Ipres (Ypres)

Old Tom
8 Grote Markt; tel: 057 20 15 41; www.oldtom.be; €–€€; daily noon–2.30pm, 6–9pm, café 7.30am–11pm; bus: 84 from Ieper station; map p.138 B1

A classic address on the Grote Markt, this hotel-bistro is favoured by Ypres locals as well as guests staying in its hotel rooms upstairs. Tasty Belgian classics like shrimp croquettes, mussels and eels are served in professional and friendly style, although service can be slow when the terrace gets busy on sunny days.

Ostend

BELGIAN
Beluga
Kemmelbergstraat 33; tel: 059 51 15 88; www.belugaoostende.be; €€; daily noon–3pm, 6–10pm; bus: 5 from Ostend station; map p.138 B3

Stylish bar-restaurant on the Ostend promenade that specialises in seafood with a French-Belgian theme, and serves anything from simple onion soup to Belgian caviar. Warm, welcoming and a bit more special inside than most other seafront addresses, although the food is still a fair price.

Villa Maritza
Albert Promenade I 76; tel: 059 50 88 08; www.villa-maritza.be; €€€; Tue–Sun noon–2pm, Tue–Sat 7–10pm; bus: 5 from Ostend station; map p.138 B3

In a class of its own: a listed monument with a sea view from the elevated ground floor and with no terrace outside. It has no need of passing trade: the gastronomic menu is seasonally inspired and original, the service formal and its reputation well-established.

Below: the coast is the place to go for the freshest seafood.

Shopping

Bruges has a reputation for twee boutiques selling chocolate and lace, and there is no shortage of these, but there are also plenty of stylish shops in this small town. Belgians are not, generally, won over by the 'pile 'em high, sell 'em cheap' type of retail experience; they like to shop at leisure in pleasant surroundings with attentive service. As a result, the small, specialist boutique and family-run retailer continues to thrive here. Note that shops for chocolate, beer, books, CDs and beauty products are covered, respectively, under *'Food and Drink', 'Literature and Theatre', 'Music and Dance',* and *'Pampering'.*

The Shopping Map

Lace and chocolate shops *(see p.125 and p.59)* and other stores catering to tourists are concentrated on the well-worn groove between the Burg, Markt and Begijnhof, along **Breidelstraat**, **Wollestraat** and **Katelijnestraat**.

The main shopping area is located west of the Markt. The familiar chains, including Belgian department store, Inno, are found along **Steenstraat** and **Zuidzandstraat**, which runs from the Markt to 't Zand. The more fashionable boutiques are located in the parallel streets of **Geldmuntstraat** and **Noordzandstraat**, and in the **Zilverpand** shopping precinct, situated between Noordzandstraat and Zuidzandstraat. **Vlamingstraat**, to the north of the Markt, also has some good stores.

Department Stores

Galeria Inno
Steenstraat 11–13; tel: 050 33 06 03; www.inno.be; Mon–Sat 9.15am–6pm; bus: 0/Centrum; map p.134 C4
The Bruges branch of Belgium's premier department

store, good for fashion, perfumery and accessories.

Design and Interiors

De Ark van Zarren
Zuidzandstraat 19; tel: 050 33 77 28; www.arkvanzarren.be; Mon–Fri 10am–6.30pm, Sat 9.30am–6.30pm, Sun in Feb school holiday and Easter–Dec 3–6.30pm; bus: 0/Centrum; map p.134 B3
Charming homeware store packed with romantic linens and accessories. The owners run a similarly stylish guesthouse near Diksmuide, towards Ypres.

Au Bonheur des Dames
Hoogstraat 38; tel: 050 33 63 63; www.desdames.be; Tue–Sat 10.30am–6pm; map p.135 D4
Beautiful store whose owner Sophie Verlinde has a talent for displaying floral fabrics, beads, glassware, picture frames and other items.

Callebert
Wollestraat 25; tel: 050 33 50 61; www.callebert.be; Tue–Sat 10am–noon, 2–6pm, Sun–Mon 3–6pm; bus: 0/Centrum, 1; map p.134 C4
Sleek interiors shop selling a striking selection of glassware, cutlery and furniture by some

of Europe's best designers. There is even a kids' section for style-conscious parents. On the first floor is the Artonivo design centre and gallery (daily 3–6pm; free), which hosts frequent exhibitions of local designer craft items.

Dille & Kamille
Simon Stevinplein 17–18; tel: 050 34 11 80; www.dille-kamille.be; Mon–Sat 9.30am–6.30pm, Sun 11am–6.30pm; bus: 0/Centrum, 1; map p.134 B3
Bruges branch of the Dutch homeware store that has won

Below: Dille & Kamille on Stevinplein for homeware.

Left: local designers Delvaux create luxurious leather goods.

Ann Demeulemeester, AF Vandevorst and Bruno Pieters, jewellery by Antwerp's own Wouters and Hendrix, and a small menswear section with items by Van Noten, among others.

Olivier Strelli
Eiermarkt 3; tel: 050 34 38 37; www.strelli.be; Mon–Fri 10am–6pm, Sat 10am–6.30pm; bus: 0/Centrum; map p.134 B4

The Brussels designer has established a loyal following in Bruges, with this large shop selling womenswear, and a smaller menswear branch nearby (Geldmuntstraat 19, tel: 050 33 26 75). Collections range from smart-casual to evening-wear; he also has a bedding line.

Rue Blanche
Simon Stevinplein 16; tel: 050 34 79 38; www.rueblanche.com; Mon–Sat 10.15am–1pm, 1.30–6pm; bus: 0/Centrum; map p.134 B3

This Belgian womenswear brand launched in Brussels producing knitwear in the late 1980s, but has expanded to a complete collection of tailored dresses and separates, whose unstructured, feminine style evoke French bohemian chic.

Jewellery and Accessories

Brugs Diamanthuis
Cordoeaniersstraat 5 (off Philipstockstraat); tel: 050 34 41 60; www.diamondhouse.net; Mon–Sat 10am–6pm, sometimes also Sun; bus: 0/Centrum; map p.134 C4

In a beautiful building dating from 1518, this shop sells a sparkling array of fine diamond jewellery designed and produced by local craftspeople. The proprietors – a Danish-Turkish couple who met

---

If you are looking for a bargain, the magic words to look for on shop windows are *Solden* (Sales) and *Totale Uitverkoop* (Everything Must Go). Visitors from non-EU countries may be able to claim back value-added tax (BTW) on purchases in some shops; look for a sticker on the window or door. It is worth asking, particularly if you buy expensive items.

---

a faithful following for its country-style kitchen utensils, table linen, wooden toys and gifts, soaps, teas, dried flowers and plants. Reasonably priced and good for gifts.

G & M Pollentier – Maréchal
Sint-Salvatorskerkhof 8; tel: 050 33 18 04; Tue–Fri 2–6pm, Sat 10am–noon, 2–6pm, Sun 10.30am–12.30pm and by appointment; bus: 0/Centrum; map p.134 B3

Tucked behind Sint-Salvatorskathedraal, this antique print and map shop owned by Geert Pollentier also does framing. It may be the only place in Bruges to sell the 1562 Marcus Gerards map of

Bruges (see the original in the Stadhuis, *p.81*). Prints date from the 18th–20th century, and include, on occasion, the work of Felicien Rops, a decadent *fin-de-siècle* artist from Namur. If the shop looks shut, the owner may be upstairs working on a framing job, so try later or ring the bell.

Fashion
It will not take you long to notice that the Flemings like to keep up appearances, both at home – see the neat-as-a-pin houses, with their window boxes and café curtains? – as well as in person: well-groomed and well-dressed, they are rightly proud of the recent generation of Belgian fashion designers who have achieved world renown.

L'Héroine
Noordzandstraat 32; tel: 050 33 56 57; www.lheroine.be; Mon–Sat 10am–6.30pm; bus: 0/Centrum; map p.134 B4

A striking boutique with clothes by top Flemish fashion designers, as well as hip international brands like Acne and Rick Owens. Womenswear by Dries Van Noten,

Above: the window display of the Tintin shop on Steenstraat.

through the diamond trade and moved to Bruges over 20 years ago – also run the Diamantmuseum on Katelijnestraat *(see p.84)*.

Delvaux
Breidelstraat 2; tel: 050 49 01 31; www.delvaux.be; Mon–Sat 10am–6pm, Dec also Sun 2–5.30pm; bus: 0/Centrum; map p.134 C4
Brussels family firm Delvaux has been working leather since 1829. Today, young designers keep the tradition alive in luxurious bags, gloves, scarves and leather jewellery.

Optique Hoet
Vlamingstraat 19; tel: 050 33 50 02; www.hoet.be; Mon–Fri 9am–6.30pm, Sat 9am–6pm; bus: 0/Centrum; map p.134 C4
Bruges family firm of opticians and eyewear designers. The Hoet label frames are limited edition and made of horn, stainless steel, titanium or gold. There are more wacky frames under the Theo brand.

Markets

Antiques and Flea Market
Dijver, with an extension at the Vismarkt; 15 Mar–15 Nov Sat–Sun 10am–6pm; bus: 0/Centrum; map p.134 C3
In addition to being a source of bargains and fine antiques,

the market stalls' scenic setting beside the tree-shaded canal makes this also a treat for the eyes.

Fish Market, Vismarkt
Tue–Sat mornings; bus: 6, 16; map p.135 C4
A limited number of fishmongers' stalls set up most mornings in the elegant 1820s colonnaded market. Worth taking a look to identify the numerous species of fish, supplied that morning fresh from Zeebrugge and Ostend. The market area is occupied by wooden toy and craft stalls at other times.

Markt
Wed 8am–1pm; bus: 0/Centrum; map p.134 C4

For a small country, Belgium's fashion design roster is impressive; most trained at Antwerp's renowned Fine Arts Academy or Brussels' La Cambre school. Belgium's Fashion darlings include **Dries Van Noten**, **Ann Demeulemeester**, **Diane von Furstenberg**, **Martin Margiela** (formerly head designer at Hermes), **Raf Simons** (creative director at Jil Sander), **Olivier Theyskens** (ex-artistic director of Nina Ricci and formerly of Rochas).

General market set in the square built for the purpose many centuries ago.

't Zand and Beursplein
Sat 8am–1pm; bus: 0/Centrum; map p.134 A3
General market selling food and other goods.

Souvenirs

Lace was once the principal product made in Bruges and is certainly the premier souvenir today. While most lace on sale is machine-made, usually in the Far East, genuine hand-made lace can still be found, and some shops deal only in the hand-made product (while most sell a mix of the two). You can frequently watch ladies making lace items in the shops and the Lace Centre runs courses to train aspiring lace-makers. Hand-made lace is expensive: a large wedding veil or tablecloth costs upwards of €400.

Other Belgian products to look for, though most of them are not specific to Bruges, include modern **tapestries**, **diamonds**, **ceramics**, **crystal** (especially the hand-blown products of the Val-Saint-Lambert workshop in Liège), **jewellery** from respected modern designers based

One of the best things about shopping in Belgium is that most shops offer a complimentary gift-wrapping service. Even at the busiest times of year, sales assistants will take their time to complete a beautiful presentation for one customer, finished with ribbons and bows: infuriating if you are in the queue and in a hurry, but if you are not it can make the experience a real pleasure. Remember to say that your purchase is for a gift when you are buying it.

Below: shop in the Belgian fashion stores, stock up on souvenirs or browse the markets.

mostly in Antwerp and Brussels, and, if you can find them, **pewter** from Huy and hand-beaten **copper** or **bronze**, Dinanderie, from Dinant in the Meuse Valley.

LACE SHOPS
Several shops claim to be the only one selling hand-made lace, but this is not the case. Here is our selection:

't Apostelientje
Balstraat 11; tel: 050 33 78 60; Tue 1–5pm, Wed–Sat 9.30am–12.15pm, 1.15–5pm, Sun 10am–1pm; bus: 6, 16; map p.133 D1
A small boutique and craft-shop just around the corner from the Kantcentrum (Lace Centre, see p.89), its owners insist on the real thing; all hand made by local women. You can look at specimens of old lace as well as stock up on supplies to try your hand at the craft yourself.

Claeys Antique
Katelijnestraat 54; tel: 050 33 98 19; www.claeysantique.com; Mon–Sat 9am–6pm; bus: 1; map p.134 C2
Specialists in antique lace since 1980, also selling antique jewellery. Antwerp-born owner Diane Claeys was born into a family of lacemakers and grew passionate about the craft, authoring several books on the subject. She has forged strong ties with Japan, where she frequently lectures and runs classes in lace-making. She also holds residential-courses lasting 1–3 days in her Bruges study house.

Irma
Oude Burg 4; www.irma.be; tel: 050 33 59 01; daily 10am–5.30pm; bus: 0/Centrum; map p.134 C4
One of the few addresses selling lace hand made in Belgium: new or antique designs, in everything from handkerchiefs, tiny designs in frames

and pendants, or large tray- and tablecloths. A variety of traditional designs are available off-the-shelf or to order. On certain days there is a lace-maker in action demonstrating the bobbin-lace method.

Kantuweeltje
Philipstockstraat 11; tel: 050 33 42 25; daily 10am–6pm; bus: 0/Centrum; map p.134 C4
A hand-made lace and tapestry specialist since 1895, where you can also watch lace being made by hand.

Unusual Gifts
Museum shop
Dijver 16; Tue–Sun 10am–6pm; bus: 0/Centrum; map p.134 C4
Located in a former stable building in the courtyard opposite the Arentshuis, the city-run museum shop has an inspired selection of art books, jewellery, watches, games, postcards, posters and children's art books. One example is a satchel decorated with a Bosch triptych.

The Tintin Shop
Steenstraat 3; tel: 050 33 42 92; www.tintinshopbrugge.be; Mon–Sat 9.30am–6pm, Sun 11am–6pm; bus: 0/Centrum; map p.134 C4
Not only books featuring the eponymous Belgian comic book hero and his little dog Snowy – but T-shirts, children's clothing, books, cards, DVDs, scale models – including a red-and-white-chequered Moon rocket – and jigsaw puzzles.

De Witte Pelikaan
Vlamingstraat 23; tel: 050 34 82 84; Mon–Sat 10am–5.30pm, mid-Nov–Christmas also Sun 10am–5.30pm; bus 0/Centrum; map p.134 C4
It is Santa Claus (or Sinter klaas) time all year round in this specialist Christmas shop, which sells tasteful tree decorations, garlands, teddies and accessories.

125

Transport

Close proximity to channel ports and an excellent national rail network put Bruges within easy reach of neighbouring countries and the Belgian capital, Brussels, which has extensive international transport links. This chapter outlines the main ways of reaching the city, as well as how to get around once there. Navigating the compact centre should be done on foot or by bike; although little of Bruges is officially car-free, driving is strongly discouraged: there are few parking spaces and most streets are one-way only. If you do arrive by car, this section gives details of where to park it.

Getting There

AIR

Most international airlines fly into Brussels Airport at Zaventem, just outside Brussels. Beneath the airport is a railway station, with direct trains to Brussels and Ghent. The journey to Bruges involves one change at Brussels North and takes 1 hr 30 mins. Brussels Airport (tel: 0900 700 00 [Belgium], +32 2 753 7753 [elsewhere]; www.brusselsairport.be).

Taken together, British Airways, bmi, Flybe and Brussels Airlines operate virtually an hourly day service between Brussels and London – less frequently from other cities around Britain. Aer Lingus and Brussels Airlines fly between Dublin and Brussels. There are direct daily flights from many cities in North America and Canada, among them New York, Washington, Chicago, Atlanta and Toronto.

Ryanair flies from Glasgow, Dublin and Shannon to Brussels Charleroi, from where charter coaches ferry passengers to and from Brussels in around 1 hr (Voy-

Above: Bruges is well connected by rail to the rest of Belgium.

ages Lelan, tel: 071 35 33 15; www.voyages-lelan.be; or buy a ticket on the bus).

Nearby Ostend airport, www.ost.aero, is used principally by cargo traffic or charter flights to Mediterranean resorts.

CAR

Bruges is located on the E40 motorway linking London with Istanbul. Drivers from Britain can travel through the Channel Tunnel on the Eurotunnel from Folkestone to Calais, a drive-on, drive-off train service that

takes 35 mins, or about 1 hr from motorway to motorway. You can just turn up and buy a ticket, but it is worth booking ahead at busy times of the year to avoid a wait. Payment is made at toll booths, which accept cash, cheques or credit cards. The price applies to the car, regardless of the number of passengers or car size. Eurotunnel, (tel: 0990 353 535 [UK], www.eurotunnel.com). The service runs 24 hrs a day, all year, with up to five departures an hour, depending on the season and time of day.

Left: most people arrive in Bruges by train.

anteed a seat. (For timetables and reservations, see www.euro star.com or tel: 08705 186 186; from outside UK, tel: +44 1233 617 575. Note that there is a £5 charge for booking by phone.)

Fast intercity trains (IC) from Brussels to Bruges are modern and comfortable, with toilets but no refreshments. They are often crowded at weekends and in the summer. The main station lies just outside the old city. It takes about 10 mins to walk into town; the central shuttle bus from the station to the Markt is number 0/Centrum.

Aviation is 10 times more damaging to the climate than other forms of transport. To neutralise their emissions, many people choose to 'carbon-offset', an effort to balance the CO2 emissions of their journey through investing in a product that saves or stores an equivalent amount of carbon dioxide. Several organisations exist to calculate the CO2 cost of your journey, collect your donation and invest in renewable energy projects in developing countries. Two good organisations are Atmosfair (www.atmosfair.de) and Pure (www.puretrust.org. uk). But remember: offsetting does not reduce emissions or prevent climate change.

From Calais, allow 1 hr 20 mins to drive to Bruges. From the E40, follow signs to Brugge Centrum for the centre of town.

COACH

A cheap way to travel to Bruges is by coach. National Express Eurolines runs one service daily from London (Victoria Coach Station) to Bruges, en route to Amsterdam. The journey takes about 5½ hrs. There are discounts for young people and senior citizens, and the ticket includes the crossing via Eurotunnel. (For more information and to book Eurolines; tel: 08717 81 81 81 [UK; daily 8am–8pm]; www.eurolines.co.uk; from Belgium tel: 02 274 13 50.)

RAIL

Bruges lies on the main railway line connecting Brussels with Ghent and the Belgian coast. Trains from Brussels to Bruges take just under 1 hr. For train times, see the Belgian railway SNCB/NMBS website (www.b-rail.be).

You can travel from London (St Pancras) or Kent (Ebbsfleet or Ashford) to Brussels by Eurostar in under 2 hrs. The service runs up to 10 times a day, and your ticket will include free onward travel on Belgian railways to Bruges (within 24 hrs of the time stamped on the Eurostar ticket). There are reduced fares for children aged 4–11; those aged 3 and under travel free but are not guar-

SEA

Cross-Channel ferries from the UK serve French and Belgian sea-ports within easy reach of Bruges by car.

P&O Ferries and Seafrance serve the busy Dover-Calais route, each operating over 20 ferries daily; crossings take 90 mins. (P&O, tel: 08705 980 333, www.poferries.com; Seafrance, tel: 0871 663 2546, www.seafrance. com.) Calais is 120km (75 miles) from Bruges and the

Below: parking in the centre of town is a nightmare.

127

journey by car takes around 1 hr 20 mins.

Ferries from Dover to Dunkirk are operated by Norfolkline, which runs about 11 crossings each way daily, taking 2 hrs. (Contact or book on tel: 0870 870 10 20; www.norfolkline.com.) Dunkirk is closer to Bruges – 76km (47 miles) – and the drive takes just under 1 hr.

Transeuropa Ferries operates up to four crossings daily from Ramsgate to Ostend, with a journey time of 4 hrs (tel: 01843 595522; www.transeuropaferries.co.uk). Ostend is 30km (18 miles) from Bruges.

P&O Ferries also runs a nightly service from Hull to Zeebrugge (every other night in Jan), which takes around 12 hrs. Zeebrugge is 17km (10 miles) from Bruges. And Norfolkline schedules three departures a week from Scotland (Rosyth) to Zeebrugge, with a journey time of around 18 hrs.

Getting Around

ORIENTATION

Bruges is a compact town with all the main sights, hotels and restaurants located within the line of medieval ramparts (demarcated today by the ring canal). When looking for an address, it is helpful to know that a *reie* is a canal, a *plaats* or *plein* is a square and a *straat* is a street. If you are navigating without a map, the easiest way to get to the cen-

Two Bruges-based companies organise tours to Ieper (Ypres) and the World War I battlefields: Quasimodo: (not to be confused with bike tour company QuasiMundo; *see box, right*; Kapellestraat 87, 8020 Oostkamp; tel: 050 37 04 70; www.quasimodo.be) and Flanders Fields Battlefield Daytours (tel: 050 34 60 60; www.visitbruges.org).

tre is to look for the octagonal top of the belfry. Elsewhere in town, church spires provide useful landmarks.

BUSES

Most places in Bruges are easily reached on foot, although you may want to take a bus from the station to the town centre. The city and its suburbs are served by a network of small buses operated by Flemish public transport company De Lijn. The 0/Centrum route runs from the station to the 't Zand, the Markt and back; all other buses also serve this route. A single ticket bought on the bus costs €1.60 from the driver (€1.20 if purchased in advance from a shop or ticket booth) and is valid for 1 hr including any change of bus within the Bruges zone. Cheaper options include a day pass (€6 or €5 in advance), or a 10-journey pass, which can be used on buses and trams throughout Flanders (€8); these passes are available at the ticket booth. Tickets have to be inserted in the orange scanner near the doors every time you board a bus.

De Lijn buses serve pretty much every town and village in Flanders and are very reliable. To plan trips out of town, the 'routeplanner' function at the com-

Below: one of the best ways to see Bruges is by bicycle; for details on renting a bike, *see right*.

Above: a row of Citroen 2CVs in Bruges for a rally.

pany's website is very useful, but does require a rudimentary grasp of Dutch: www.delijn.be.

CAR

Parking within Bruges centre is almost impossible and navigation is difficult because of the network of one-way streets. Most tourists are advised by their hotels to leave their vehicles at the large car park next to the station (Stationsplein) in the south-west corner of the city, which has space for 1,500 cars (cheapest, and includes free bus ride into town), or in one of four other underground car parks in the old town. Some hotels have limited parking, but charges are usually high. For the station car park, claim a free public transport ticket for each person in the car by presenting your car park ticket at the office of De Lijn, the bus company operator, located outside the railway station, and telling them how many people are travelling in the car.

CYCLING

It is clear as soon as you arrive that Bruges is a city of cyclists. Although everywhere is within walking dis-

tance, a bike allows you to cover a lot of distance in a short time, for a ride around the ramparts, to take in the outlying districts, or for a trip out of town. The most popular trip is along the tree-lined Daamsevaart canal to the charming little town of Damme, which is not well-served by buses. Take the minor road on the north side of the canal to avoid the traffic, which takes the road along the southern bank.

Several shops hire bikes by the hour, day or week. The most convenient option for those coming on a day ticket by train (and without luggage) is to rent a bike directly at the station, as you can get a combined train and bike rental ticket. The following places provide bicycle hire.

B-Bike
't Zand 34 (Concertgebouw); tel: 0479 97 12 80; www.b-bike.be

Bruges railway station
Tel: 050 30 23 29; map p.134 B1

Eric Popelier
Mariastraat 26; tel: 050 34 32 62; www.fiietsenpopelier.be; map p.134 C3

QuasiMundo
Nieuwe Gentweg 5; tel: 050 33 07 75; www.quasimundo.com; map p.134 C2

't Koffiieboontje
Hallenstraat 4; tel: 050 33 80 27; www.hotel-koffiieboontje.be; map p.134 C4

Bauhaus Bike Rental
Langestraat 145; tel: 050 34 10 93; www.bauhaus.be; map p.133 E1

Snuffel Backpacker Hostel
Ezelstraat 47-49; tel: 050 33 31 33; www.snuffel.be; map p.132 B1

WALKING

The compact scale of Bruges and the quasi absence of cars make it an ideal city for strolling around. It takes approximately 20 mins to walk from the railway station to the main square. The tourist office has mapped out four walks within the city. The walks are described in English on the website www.brugge.be.

> Companies that organise guided bike tours in and around Bruges include: **QuasiMundo Bike Tours**, Nieuwe Gentweg 5; tel: 050 33 07 75; www.quasimundo.com; **Pink Bear Bicycle Company**; tel: 050 61 66 86, www.pinkbear.freeservers.com; **The Green Bike Tour**; tel: 050 61 26 67; www.amusementvlaanderen.be.

Atlas

The following streetplans of Bruges and Ghent makes it easy to find the attractions listed in our A–Z section. A selective index to streets and sights will help you find other locations throughout the city.

Map Legend

	Pedestrian area	✈ ✈	Airport / airfield
	Notable building	🚢	Car ferry
	Park	🚌	Bus station
	Hotel	ⓘ	Tourist information
	Urban area	⊕	Hospital
	Non urban area	🎏	Windmill
+ +	Cemetery	🗼	Lighthouse
	Railway	⊞	Cathedral / church
)┈┈(	Tunnel	✡	Synagogue
⊢+⊣	Canal	1	Statue / monument
– – –	Ferry route	✉	Post Office

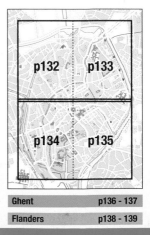

| p132 | p133 |
| p134 | p135 |

Bruges

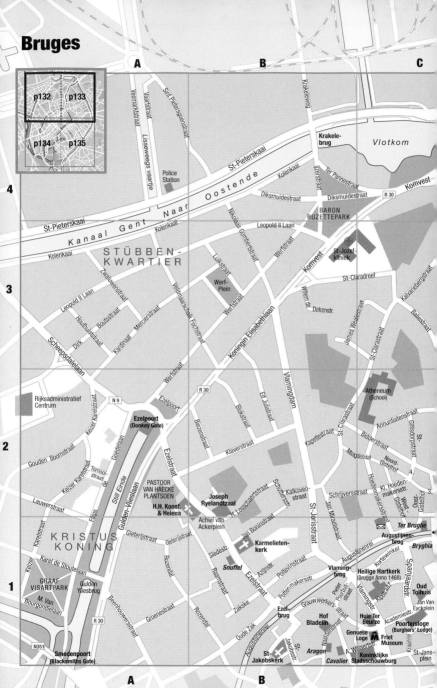

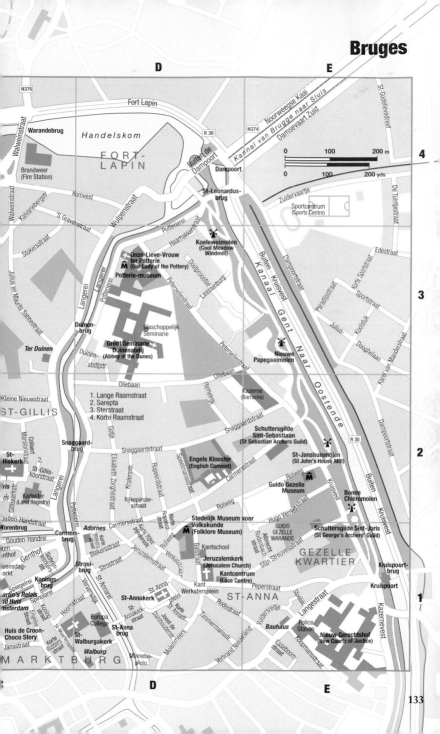

Bruges

Bruges

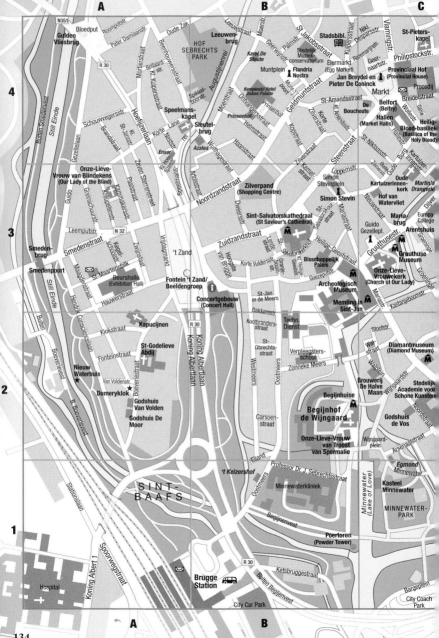

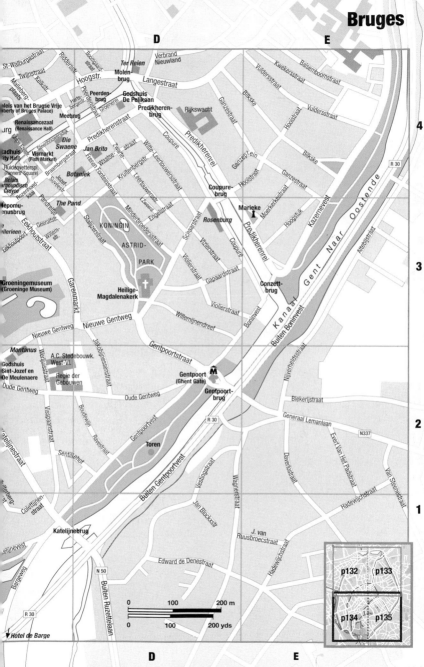

St-Walburgastraat
Twijnstraat
Kelkstraat
Mariebergplaats
aleis van het Brugse Vrije (Liberty of Bruges Palace)
Renaissancezaal (Renaissance Hall)
urg
adhuis (City Hall)
Huidenvettersplein (Tanners' Square)
Belois argoudisch-Crayer
Nepomuenusbrug
illerieen
Eekhoutstraat Willem-str.
Lekhoudpoort Geerolfstr.
Pandreitje
Groeningemuseum (Groeninge Museum)

Rodderstr.
Boomgaard straat
Peerdenbrug Paardenstraat Groenerei
Meebrug
Predikherenstraat
Die Swaene
Jan Brito Steenhouwersdijk
Vismarkt (Fish Market)
Botanlek Braambergstraat
Jozef Suvée-str.
The Pand
Geerolfstr.
Garenmarkt

Ter Reien
Hoogstr. Molenbrug
Godshuis De Pelikaan
Predikheren-brug

Langestraat
Verbrand Nieuwland

Hertsbergestr. Zwarte straat Witte-Leertouwersstr.
Vrijen Waatsc. Krutenbergstr.
Freren Fonteinstraat Leertouwersstr.
Eiewz.
Minderbroedersstraat
Staalijzerstraat
Engelstraat

Predikherenrei
Coupure
Coupure-brug
Marieke
Rosenburg
Schaarstraat
Vizierstraat
Violierstraat
Gapaardstraat

Rijkswacht

Ganzestraat
Ganzenplein
Hooistraat
Ganzestraat

Kwekersstraat Balsemboomstraat
Vuldersstraat
Bilkse Vuldersstraat
Moerkerkestraat Hoogstuk
Kazernevest

KONINGIN ASTRID-PARK

Heilige-Magdalenakerk

Nieuwe Gentweg
Nieuwe Gentweg

Coupure
Willemijnendreef
Violierstraat
Bonivest

Conzett-brug

Montanus
Godshuis Sint-Jozef en De Meulenaere
Oude Gentweg
Werfjusstraat
Visspaanstraat

A.C. Stedebouwk. West-Vl.
Regie der Gebouwen
Jakobijnessenstraat
Gentpoortstraat
Oude Gentweg
Boudewijn Renesstraat
Sentillehot
Coblentiestraat

Gentpoort (Ghent Gate)
Gentpoort-brug
Gentpoortvest
Toren
Buiten Gentpoortvest
Jan Blockstr.
Vestingstraat
Wagnerstraat

Blekerijstraat
Generaal Lemanlaan
N337
Nijverheidsstraat

K a n a a l   G e n t   N a a r   O o s t e n d e
R 30
Buiten Bonivrest
Attebijlestraat

Dayerlostraat
Evert Van Het Padstraat
Van Steenstraat
Hadewijchstraat

Katelijnebrug
Buiten Ruzettelaan
R 30
Bargeweg
elijnevest
Coilettiene-straat

Edward de Denestraat
N 50
J. van Ruusbroecstraat
Hadewijchstraat

↓ *Hotel de Barge*

| 0 | 100 | 200 m |
| 0 | 100 | 200 yds |

p132 p133
p134 p135

135

Ghent

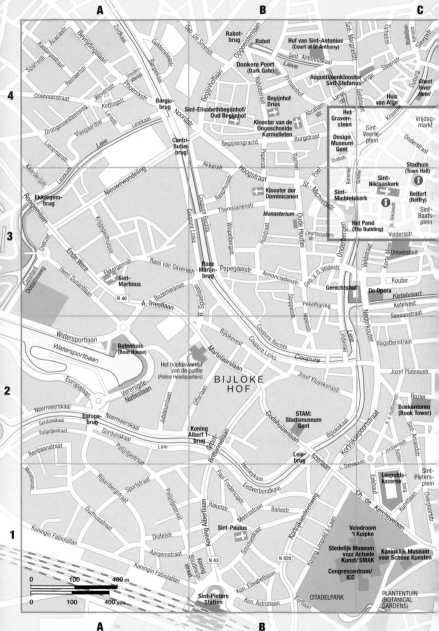

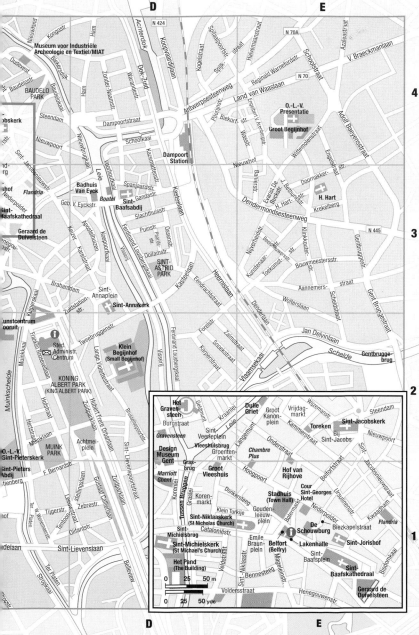

Ghent

N 424

N 70A

N 70

V. Braeckmanlaan

Azalealaan

Adolf Baeyensstraat

Engelst.

Kongostr.

Ham

Achterdok

Koopvaardijlaan

Dok-Zuid

Zonder-Naamstr.

Warandestr.

Kogelstraat

Spijk.

Spitaalpoortstr. straat

Reginald Warnefordstr.

Schoolstraat

Halvemaanstraat

Nieuwevest

Blekersdijk

Baudelokaai

Oudevest

Baudelost.

4

BAUDELO PARK

Steendam

Nieuwpoort

Dampoortstraat

Schoolkaai

Nieuwbrugkaai

Voorhoutkaai

Kazernestr.

Dampoort Station

Nieuwhof

Antwerpsesteenweg

Land van Waaslaan

Engelbert V. Arenbergstr.

Pijndersstr.

Biekorf- str.

Bannerstr.

O.-L.-V. Presentatie

Groot Begijnhof

Wittemolenstraat

obskerk

ind-
rg

hof

Flandria

Nederpolder

Badhuis Van Eyck

Boatel

Sint-Baafsabdij

Geb. V. Eyckstr.

Spanjaardstr.

Gandastr.

Slachthuisstr.

Kasteellaan

Evarist De
Buck
J. Bethun-
estr.

Doornakker-str.

H. Hart-
str.

Krekelberg

H. Hart

N 445

Sint-
aafskathedraal

Geraard de Duivelsteen

negou-
str.

Leie

Keizer

Apostelhuizen

Korpoortkaai

Kardastraat

Visserij

Puinstr.

Pr.
str.

Paarde-
str.

Oostendr.

Dollamstr.

SINT-ASTRID PARK

Dendermondsesteenweg

Nijverheidstr.

Beschermersstr.

Kunstenaar-
str.

Bouwmeestersstr.

Toekomst-
str.

Klinkouter-
str.

Gentbruggestr.

Brabantdam

Kwaadham

Sint-
Annaplein

Zuidstation-
str.

Sint-Annakerk

Kasteellaan

Hermanstraat

Eendrachtstraat

Aannemers-
straat

Scheldstraat

Wolterslaan

Gent Brugstraat

3

Koningin
Maria Hendrikaplein

Kunstcentrum
Vooruit

Sted.
Administr.
Centrum

Klein
Begijnhof
(Small Beginhof)

Lange Violettestraat

Tweebruggenstr.

Hubert Frère Orbanlaan

Brusselsepoortstr.

Visserij

Ferdinand Lousbergskaai

Forelstr.

Zalmstraat

Snoekstraat

Karperstraat

Vlaamsekaai

Jan Delvinlaan

Schelde

Gentbrugge-
brug

2

KONING ALBERT PARK
(KING ALBERT PARK)

<!-- Inset map box -->

Het
Gravensteen

Burgstraat

Geldmunt

Kraanlei

Leie

Langemunt

Dulle
Griet

Groot
Kanon-
plein

Vrijdag-
markt

Wijzemansstr.

Kammerstraat

Steendam

Toreken

Bij
Sint-Jacobs

Sint-Jacobskerk

Nieuwpoort

Sint-Jacobsnieuwstraat

Gravensteen

Design
Museum
Gent

Sint-
Veerleplein

Vleeshuisbrug

Groenten-
markt

Chambre
Plus

Onderstraat

Hof van
Rijhove

Belfortstraat

Franklin Rooseveltlaan

Kortrijksepoortstr.

Achtermei-
plein

MUINK
PARK

Muinkschelde

Muinkkaai

Hofstraat

Stellingstraat

Holstraat

F. Bernardstr.

Zuidparklaan

Grasbrug

Korenlei

Tussen Bruggen

Graslei

Koren-
markt

Marriott
Ghent

Groot
Vleeshuis

Donkersteeg

Klein Turkije

Gouden-
leeuw-
plein

Stadhuis
(Town Hall)

Botermarkt

Cour
Sint-Georges
Hotel

Nederpolder

Ursulinenstr.

De
Schouwburg

Biezekapelstraat

Flandria

O.-L.-V.
Sint-Pieterskerk

Sint-Pieters
Abdij

tienberg

Sint-
Michielsbrug

Sint-Michielskerk
(St Michael's Church)

Het Pand
(The Building)

Cataloniëstr.

Sint-Niklaaskerk
(St Nicholas Church)

Emile
Braun-
plein

Veldstraat

Sint-Niklaasstr.

Belfort
(Belfry)

Lakenhalle

Magoleinstr.

Sint-
Baafsplein

Sint-Jorishof

Sint-
Baafskathedraal

Geraard de
Duivelsteen

0   25   50 m

0   25   50 yds

hof

Tijgerstr.

Tentoonst.

Sint-Lievenslaan

Ter W. Wemmerstr.

Olifantstr.

Ter Platen

Leeuwstraat

Gustaaf Callierlaan

Zebrestr.

Bellevue

Voldersstraat

Bennesteg

Henegouwenstr.

delaan

stroppkaai

Ter Platen

Stropkaai

Sint-Lievenslaan

1

137

Flanders

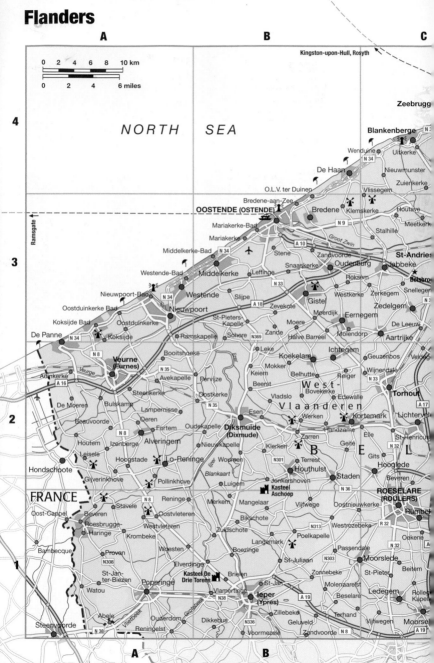

Flanders

Index

Insight Smart Guide: Bruges
Compiled by: Katharine Mill
Edited by: Joanna Potts/Scarlett O'Hara
Proofread and indexed by: Penny Phenix
Photography by: Adornes 70tl, 70tr,
70br; AFP/Getty Images 63tr; Age
Fotostock/Superstock 100; AKG
Images 62tr, 63c, 75b; AKG
Images/Erich Lessing 60b, 96b; The
Art Archive/Galleria degli Uffizi Flo-
rence/Dagli Orti 96-97tc; Bettman/
Corbis 60t; B-In 94-95tc; John Brun-
ton 28-29tc; Chris Coe/Apa 81b; Concertgebouw Croquet-Zouridakis 18,
38-39tc; Jan Darthet 81t; Jerry Den-
nis/APA 4t, 5tl, 5c, 5b, 9t, 10, 13t,
15b, 22-23, 26b, 27b, 29b, 35t, 38b,
39b, 40, 41, 47b, 50, 51, 59, 72-73tc,
78-79tc, 79b, 80t, 84bl, 101, 105b,
107t, 125c, 130t, 132-133; Daniël de
Kievith 16, 21t, 21b; De Reyghere
76b; De Tuilerieen 66t, 66b; Die
Swaene 64b; Glyn Genin/APA back
cover t & b, 2-3tc, 2b, 3b, 5tr, 5cl, 5cr,
6, 7t, 7b, 8, 9b, 24b, 28b, 30b, 31b,
32, 33t, 33b, 34t, 36b, 37, 43b, 45bl,
45br, 46-47tc, 48, 49, 52b, 45-55tc,
55b, 56-57tc, 57b, 58, 68, 73b, 78b,
80b, 84br, 90b, 104-105tc, 110, 114t,
114c, 114b, 116, 117, 120, 122-
123tc, 122b, 124, 125t, 125b, 126b,
127b, 128bl, 128br, 129; Getty
Images 63bl; Global View 25b; Jean
Godecharle 99b; Groeningemuseum,
Bruges, Belgium/The Bridgeman Art
Library 82-83tc; Groeningemuseum,

Bruges, Belgium, Giraudon/The
Bridgeman Art Library 85; Tony Halli-
day/APA 13b, 14, 15t, 17b, 20, 44,
106, 107b; Hotel Jan Brito 67; iStock-
photo 119; Britta Jaschinski/APA
34bl, 34br, 35b, 36t, 95b, 118; Bob
Krist/Corbis 30-31tc; Laif 111b; Joris
Luyten 56b; Mary Evans Picture
Library 60c, 62tl, 62cr, 62b, 74b;
Francis G Mayer/Corbis 89b; A
Nowitz/APA 108-109tc, 121; PA Pho-
tos 63br; The Pand 65b; The Print
Collector/Alamy 61br, 88; Stan Rip-
pel/iStockphoto 126-127tc; Roger-
Viollet/Topfoto 63tl, 74-75tc; Ronald
Grant Archive 77t; Scala, Florence
84t; Senses 103bl, 103br; Giovanni
Simeone/4 Corners Images 61bl; Bert
Snyders 42-43tc; Sunparks de Haan
102-103tc; Stadsfotografen, Stad
Brugge 76t; Toerisme Brugge/cel
fotografie Stad Brugge 83b, 86t, 87,
89t, 91b; Toerisme Brugge 98-99tc,
111t, 112, 113l, 113r, 115; Toerisme
Brugge/Daniel de klevith 90-91tc, 92-
93tc; Toerisme Damme 17t; Visual
Arts Library (London)/Alamy 61t, 62cl;
Walburg 69; Gregory Wrona/APA 4b,
11, 19, 24-25tc, 52-53tc, 71.
Picture Manager: Steven Lawrence
Maps: Mapping Ideas Ltd
Series Editor: Sarah Sweeney
Second Edition 2010
Reprinted 2011
© 2010 Apa Publications GmbH & Co.
Verlag KG Singapore Branch, Singapore.

Printed in Spain
Worldwide distribution enquiries:
APA Publications GmbH & Co Verlag KG
(Singapore branch); 7030 Ang Mo Kio Ave 5,
08-65 Northstar @ AMK, Singapore
569880; email: apasin@singnet.com.sg
Distributed in the UK and Ireland by:
GeoCenter International Ltd; Meridian House,
Churchill Way West, Basingstoke, Hampshire,
RG21 6YR; email: sales@geocenter.co.uk
Distributed in the United States by:
Ingram Publisher Services
One Ingram Blvd, PO Box 3006, La Vergne,
TN 37086-1986; email: customer.
service@ingrampublisherservices.com
Distributed in Australia by:
Universal Publishers; PO Box 307,
St. Leonards, NSW 1590; email:
sales@universalpublishers.com.au
Contacting the Editors
We would appreciate it if readers would alert us
to errors or outdated information by writing to:
Apa Publications, PO Box 7910, London SE1
1WE, UK; fax: (44 20) 7403 0290;
email: insight@apaguide.co.uk
No part of this book may be reproduced,
stored in a retrieval system or transmitted in
any form or by any means (electronic,
mechanical, photocopying, recording or
otherwise), without prior written permission of
Apa Publications. Brief text quotations with
use of photographs are exempted for book
review purposes only. Information has been
obtained from sources believed to be reliable,
but its accuracy and completeness, and the
opinions based thereon, are not guaranteed.

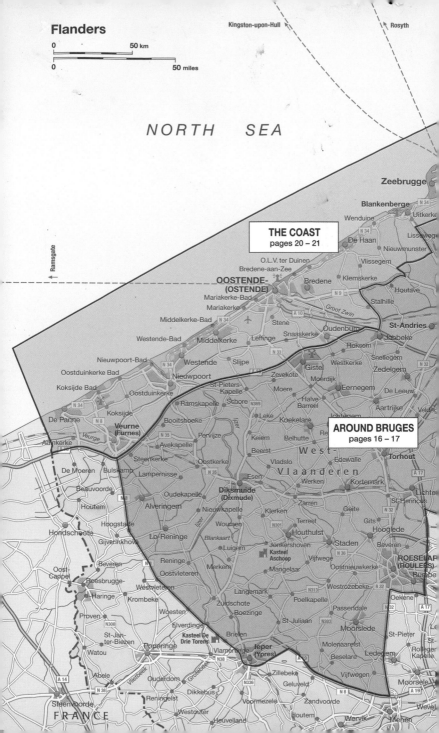